Dr. Moritz L. Gomm

How to Start a Business in 90 Days Without Quitting Your Job (yet)

Dr. Moritz L. Gomm

How to Start a Business in 90 Days

Without Quitting Your Job (yet)

The Complete Guide
from Employment to Freedom

For all those who only function,
doubt themselves and do not yet dare,
to show oneself completely.

Contents

Step 2: Create time for your business idea 121

Step 3: Discover your business idea 148

Step 4: Develop and test your business idea 168

Step 5: Do only what you like and outsource the rest 207

Step 6: Scale your business to the right size for you 227

Is it just me,
or is everybody else crazy?

*"The two most important days in your life are the day you were born and
the day you find out why."*
~ Mark Twain, US-American writer, 1835-1910

For a long time, I thought that I was not "normal." I was professionally successful,
worked at a great company in every respect, and got along well with my boss and
colleagues. The frequent positive feedback I received only served to push me even
harder to achieve the next success. It was as if I needed recognition at work as much as
I needed air to breathe.

At the beginning of 2018, I traveled to Hong Kong with my family to set up a branch
for my company, where not only was I the sole manager, but I was also the project
manager for a large banking IT project. Within one year, my branch grew to almost 20
employees.

It was an intense time. In Hong Kong's crowded underground, I answered emails
on the way to work, I took care of the project at the client's office, conducted telephone
interviews with applicants on the way home, and only put down the phone when
I unlocked the door. There my children (1 and 4 at the time) rushed to me, and I took
care of the family. When the children were in bed, I still did things for the company and
was often not in bed until after midnight.

I was successful professionally, and it was an exciting time for the whole family
in Asia. But after a year, the heavy workload and responsibility stressed me so much
that I hardly slept at night. I got panic attacks, developed depression, and unrelenting
tinnitus (ringing in the ears). I noticed that life was slowly slipping out of my fingers.
Social invitations invoked anxiety. I remember singing songs to my children at bedtime
while *simultaneously* dealing with problems at work. It was bad.

When I finally went to the doctor, he diagnosed me with chronic fatigue syndrome. I was desperate. There I was in the middle of Asia, 6,000 miles from home, with my wife and two children, solely responsible for a company. I felt at the end of my rope and just wanted to be left alone and have some peace. But I couldn't do that because I was responsible for the family and the company.

After a particularly bad night, I finally decided to pull the emergency brake and openly informed my management in Europe about my situation. They reacted in a prompt and exemplary manner. In less than four weeks, a friendly colleague moved to Hong Kong and assumed my responsibilities, which allowed me to take a holiday.

After four to eight weeks, I assumed that I would be able to work again and "step on the gas." What a mistake! It would take more than twelve months before I could work again.

At first, I took a three-month break in Hong Kong and attended therapy. After that, I started to work slowly, a few hours a day. It was frightening how little I was able to do, which was hard for me to accept. Soon afterward, we decided to return to Germany earlier than planned.

Back in Germany, I was sitting in my old office again and wanted to get started. Of course, I had decided to take it easy and not work as intensively as before. But in principle, I assumed that my body would now "work" again. Within a week, the symptoms returned, and they were stronger than before. My ears whistled and rang nonstop. It was maddening.

I realized that my body could only really "let go" after the family had returned home safely. I took sick leave, and for the first time in my life, I was prescribed psychotropic drugs. I didn't want to admit to myself that I was in such a bad way and agreed with my psychiatrist to try different alternative methods and psychotherapy. But the depression worsened, and I had problems taking care of my everyday life, not to mention work. My hopes — and those of my family — now hung on a seven-week rehab. I received round-the-clock care and met many people who were just like me: successful professionals who had their feet pulled off the ground in the middle of life.

But the worst was yet to come. When I returned home from rehab — full of hope that things would now start to improve — the depression was so bad that I had difficulty taking care of my children. It was the absolute low point of my life. On the advice of several people around me, I decided to take the prescribed antidepressants because it just couldn't get any worse.

In retrospect — only nine months ago as of this writing — that was the turning point. It took two weeks for the drug to take effect. But then, little by little, I was able to cope with everyday life again, became more stable, and fortunately didn't have any serious side effects. I was so relieved to function "normally" again and grew more positive and optimistic. Contrary to my fears, I also never had the feeling that the medication had changed me in any way or that I was not quite "me."

After taking medicine for at least six months, I slowly withdrew from it over twelve weeks. There were some mild withdrawal symptoms — especially dizziness — but the depression didn't come back.

This traumatic experience led to fundamental changes in my life. The most important and most challenging step for me was truly accepting that I had a problem with overworking and was suffering from depression. I didn't have this realization either in Asia or after the "relapse" in Germany, but only when I returned from rehab and felt the problems return even more severe than before. I believe my body had to tell me several times, each iteration more strongly, that a change was inevitable.

I decided to let go of many things that had accumulated during my life. First of all, I agreed with my employer that I would take a year off over a sabbatical. I gave up partner status with my company to be "freer" again. I canceled my membership to a professional club, where I had a great network of friends. The goal was to reduce the number of commitments I had to meet. I handed in my car and used my bicycle and car-sharing more often to reduce costs. I also decided to finally go vegetarian, which I had tried out a few times for several months but never committed.

I also began to speak openly with others about my experience and was shocked. When I shared my problems, others told me in return how badly they had been or were still feeling about their work.

Many people asked me shyly about the typical symptoms of burnout because they feared that they would experience a similar fate. That was the first time they talked to anyone about it. Good friends of mine — successful CEOs of large companies — admitted that their doctor had diagnosed them with burnout years ago, but they did not dare quit their jobs. Another friend told me that he had suffered from depression and suicidal thoughts for three years due to work.

All these people had given me the impression that they were doing well, that they were happy and prosperous. How could I have been so wrong? And how could they have successfully maintained this positive image of themselves for so long, only to tear it down so readily in our conversation? I realized that I am not "abnormal" — we all are if we make such an endless effort in our lives to ...

... to do what exactly?

Why a midlife crisis makes sense

"As long as we don't accept ourselves, we look for love in others to prove to us that we're okay."
~ Author unknown

In our childhood, we learn what is right and what is wrong from our parents, our environment, and the media. Suppose you grew up in an industrialized country like me. In that case, the ideal life is a good education that results in a job that is as prestigious and well-paid as possible, so that you can retire sometime in your mid-60s and enjoy your life.

We are "right," for example, if we are a good and obedient child, do well at school, and strive for a socially respected profession. "Wrong" is to be naughty, not to take school seriously, and to have career aspirations that clearly contradict our parents' ideas. The people who "shaped" us in this way usually meant well: We should fit into society so that we can have it easier later on.

However, if we force ourselves to live as expected by others, we suppress our inner drives and our very essence. As adults, we still have our parents' and teachers' voices in our heads: "You have to do THIS" or "It's not a decent job" or "You will never be able to be a ..." These beliefs sink deep into our subconscious and shape how we think about ourselves today as adults, what we believe we can do, and what we think we *have* to be. Among them are many helpful and useful beliefs, but unfortunately, some prevent us from living happily today.

So, we learn this formula for happiness in the first two decades of our lives, and we follow this approach for one, two, or even three decades; it's no wonder that we hit a wall in mid-life (for me, it was age 45) that, "Hmm, I've been following what I was taught for half a lifetime, and yet the promised feeling of happiness and contentment has still not materialized."

This raises the legitimate question: If it hasn't worked so far, why should it suddenly work in the second half of life? That dissonance and dissatisfaction are why people question their lives midway and think about what they *really* want to do with the rest of their lives. Some try to resolve this dissonance by trying even more of the same and find themselves buying red sports cars, starting affairs, and even behaving recklessly.

When you're in this phase and dare to reveal your doubts, insecurity, vulnerability, and weaknesses to others, you'll find that people open up to you in a whole new way. I experienced this during my burnout period. Much to my surprise, showing my weakness was perceived by others as a great strength. My deep fear that I would no longer be respected or accepted afterward was utterly unfounded! Instead, I received a lot of positive feedback and recognition for my openness. And I learned a lot about what is truly going on inside other people and their experiences.

The researcher and bestselling author, Brené Brown, formulates this paradoxical experience as:

"Vulnerability is not a weakness, it is our most reliable measure of courage."[1]

A sad spectacle of happiness

As others opened up to me, I realized why their apparent happiness and success could deceive me. It was astonishing and worrying. My interlocutors invested a lot of time and energy, creating the impression that they were doing well. There was no other way to explain the gulf between how these people appeared on the outside and what they told me about their inner life. It was as if my own openness and "weakness" unveiled the curtain to reveal their weaknesses and their "spectacle of happiness."

And honestly, don't we all play this game to some degree? Our profile photos and selfies only show us at our best in beautiful places. When somebody asks, "How are you?" what's your reply? The standard answer is almost always, "I'm great!" Think about how we make an effort to tidy up and cook when guests arrive and then tell them at dinner how well our job/child/car is going. We put on a good face at work so that nobody notices our genuine frustration.

Why are we all painting the same picture? I think it's because we're ashamed. We're ashamed of not being what we think we have to be. We're not so great at our jobs; we're not the perfect parents, the understanding partners; and we are far from the impeccable people we want to be. We simply expect too much from ourselves.

And why do we expect so much from ourselves?

Because we believe that if others can succeed, and we don't, we are doing something wrong, that we are "less than." We don't recognize that our fellow human beings are not truly succeeding either, but — like us — invest a lot of effort in creating the perception of success.

That's why dealing openly with a crisis and showing weakness and vulnerability is so liberating; it relieves my counterpart of the tedious task of keeping up the facade that they are doing great. It allows others to (finally) show that they're not as well as they seem. And that is very liberating for all involved. Think about how connected and relieved you feel when someone says to you, "I feel the same way!"

As soon as we reveal ourselves, a real connection to others is established:
"Me too! I know exactly what you mean."

That's also why people who deal with their weaknesses openly and honestly are often so likable. Just think of a clown or how children are happy when adults deliberately act clumsy. The word "sympathy" is derived from the Greek "sympáthein" and means "to pity." Because others show themselves to us, we can *suffer with* them, making them sympathetic to us. Being vulnerable is also a sign of trust, which touches us and brings us closer to the other person.

So, you've probably been asking yourself for a while now: What does all this have to do with my independence? Quite simply: To Be Independent Means to Reveal Yourself. For this reason, this book focuses on two parts: How to find and reveal yourself and how to develop a business model from there that fits you and your life.

PART I
THE BASICS

This book is for people who are looking for a new orientation.

For your orientation

What is the 90-Day Program?

The 90-Day Program is a practical guide to making your dream of independence a reality with just one step per day. You'll feel what it's like to be independent and discover whether this is a fit for you — without having to quit your job (right away).

The goal of self-employment in this book is to increase overall satisfaction and happiness with your entire lifestyle — your family, partnerships, your job, and yourself. This book and its associated program are thus self-help for both life and self-employment.

Why many self-help books don't change anything — and why this one is different

Typically, self-help books require completing practical tasks at the end of each chapter necessary to achieve your goal. Often, empty areas or lines are provided to write the results directly into the book.

Most people read the assignments and plan to do them, but unfortunately, this is often never the case. Curiosity usually makes them "read on" first and then proceed in the same way for the next tasks, so that they end up doing almost nothing.

Does that sound familiar?

The reason for this is the following: When you read a book — whether you are relaxing on the sofa or on the subway — you are in "reading mode." You read the tasks and think about them, but you don't really become active at that moment. To do things energetically, you have to switch to "action mode." This is an active, upright position in a place that is really suitable for working. To successfully implement what you are reading, you have to literally position yourself for *action*.

The 90-Day Program addresses this problem by separating the tasks from the reading and applying a structured approach.

Here's how it works: Decide which day to start the 90-Day Program, and then each day you'll perform the corresponding task from Part II of this book. Each task is accompanied by the approximate time required for completion. I recommend planning time for each task the day following your reading. Perform the task in "action mode" in your notebook, on your computer, or later in the program, during personal interactions with your future customers.

Each task includes a link and a QR code to view the task with helpful supplemental information on the Internet. Registration is not necessary. The website makes it easier for you to carry out your respective task by offering the following advantages:

- I explain the 90 tasks in a short **video**, which many people prefer over a text version (which is also available).

- On the website, you will find the necessary **tools and links** required to get started. Being on the Internet will put you into "action mode," and the content provided saves you the trouble of typing out the book.

- Because I constantly update and develop tasks based on user feedback, the website provides the **latest version of the tasks**.

Accompanying Newsletter

You'll find valuable tips & tricks for your successful startup and a more fulfilling life in my free newsletter about the 90-Day Program. Register now:

www.how-employees-startup.com/newsletter

You can, of course, cancel the newsletter at any time with one click.

TIP: Start the 90-Day Program as soon as you begin reading and continue completing the tasks in parallel with the appropriate steps. This way, you will gain hands-on knowledge about how the program works, which will quickly lead to experiencing your first signs of success.

Right now, schedule a day to start the program and reserve one hour in your calendar for "Task Day 1" (you can do this today if you like). On that day, you will do the first task on p. 99.

A reminder for all the well-I-do-the-tasks-a-little-later readers: To implement these principles, it is imperative to move from reading mode to action mode. So, open your calendar and set your start date to actuate the 90-Day Program!

For whom is the 90-Day Program?

This book is for all those who are thinking of becoming self-employed. But I have developed the concept especially for people who have little time and/or money:

- **Employees** who have an idea they'd like to realize but are professionally very busy and do not (yet) dare quit their jobs. Employees often want to become self-employed because they are dissatisfied with their current job or lack purpose in their work. They suffer from an unpleasant company culture or have conflicts with superiors or team members. Others want to do something completely different after many years of a professional career because they are unhappy with their current job despite success. Such things often happen in mid-life — for good reason — as I've described above.

- **Mothers and fathers** who are either part-time or not working at all. Here the motivation is often to stand on their own feet again professionally. As a father of two small children, I know parents are faced with a challenge: How do you put forth the necessary time and effort to become self-employed without negatively impacting your family? I will show you how.

- ✔ The 90-Day Program is especially helpful to **the unemployed** because it provides meaning and structure to everyday life. Each day brings a clear and feasible task to gradually reach the goal of finding a job you love, which will earn you enough money for life.

Is the (post) Covid era a good time to start a business?

The Covid-19 pandemic affects almost all sectors and professions. Shouldn't you play it safe right now and stay employed?

On the contrary: it makes sense to act counter-cyclically. Although times of crisis are bad when you *are* self-reliant, they are ideal for *becoming* self-reliant. There are three reasons for this:

1. In times of crisis, traditional trends will be replaced by new ones. For example, people may opt for vacationing closer to home or opting for road trips over long-haul flights.

2. As an entrepreneur, you can leverage the fallout from a crisis. For example, dollars that once went to in-restaurant dining are now spent on food delivery services. Jobless qualified professionals are available for hiring or contracting at a reasonable rate. As many businesses opt to cut advertising costs, now advertising costs have decreased — what a great time for you to market your services.

3. New entrepreneurs benefit from the upturn after the crisis, enabling them to scale their business much more quickly. On the other hand, if you start up a business in a thriving economy, you'll soon run into the next inevitable crisis.

In its white paper, *The Future after Corona* (2020), the German Future Institute states: "The phase of crisis will be the most entrepreneurial time of many decades. Any time at the end or after a crisis is the time of visionaries."[2]

So, *now* is an ideal time to start!

How to get the most out of this book

By providing precise guidance and nudging you out of your comfort zone in a fun and challenging way, the 90-Day Program will give your life an exciting new direction.

The program is designed so that you can actually "pull it off" in 90 working days. That said, we are all human, and life happens. That's when it's important to take a break. There may be good reasons to take off one, two, or even three weeks. That's okay and not unusual. During critical points in this process, I will ask you whether you need a break because there is no point in doggedly continuing under pressure and then giving up completely a short time later. It's better to take a little more time and maintain continuity to reach your goal.

Before we get started, please follow these five pieces of advice:

1. **Get a nice notebook for the 90-Day Program and write down your results every day.**

   Whoever writes, stays (on). You are welcome to start the *very first* task without taking notes, but from the second task on, you'll need your notebook!

   So, hop on the Internet or visit your favorite office supply store and treat yourself to a nice notebook.

2. **Separate „Reading" and „Doing."**

   When you are in "reading mode," either make yourself comfortable somewhere (on the sofa) or use idle time (waiting for an appointment). Put yourself in a "working state" before you tackle any of the 90 tasks. Sit down at your workplace with a notebook, a pen, and your laptop in a work position. This can be your study or the kitchen table, but not the living room sofa or bathtub.

3. **Find a sparring partner.**

   Find someone willing to discuss your ideas and plans. You should trust this person and enjoy spending time with them, and they should be open, positive, and creative. This could be your partner, a parent, a sister, or a brother. If your children are older, they can also serve as sparring partners. However, friends or valued colleagues are often better suited because they are more objective. Your family is usually directly affected by your life decisions, and that may color their views.

   Your sparring partner must be positive and supportive. An incorrigible pessimist or nagger is not helpful in this respect. You can start the program without a sparring partner but try to find one in the first two weeks.

4. **You will have to summon up courage.**

   To break new ground, you need courage. You have to dare to do something completely new, to breach your comfort zone and act differently than before, and to be convicted in what you do. Your goal is to live a more autonomous and fulfilled life. You will face the risk of (temporary) failures that will teach you invaluable lessons. You will instinctively experience resistance, but trust in yourself and move forward to overcome it. By fully engaging in the process, you'll develop new-found courage and confidence over the next 90 days.

5. **You will need chutzpa and finesse.**

   To develop, test, and execute a new business idea while continuing to work your full-time job, you need creativity and a healthy dose of professional cheekiness. While this process will not harm you, sometimes, you'll have to lean out of the window to achieve your goal. For example, you will "simulate" your business idea in advance to test, without much investment and risk, whether a market exists.

   Before you make the big leap, you'll be able to determine whether self-employment is for you. You will have to step out of your comfort zone from time to time — and this is exactly what we practice in the 90-Day Program.

And here is the "Disclaimer..."

The 90 tasks will challenge you, inspire you, make you think, and move you forward. The process of significant change requires time, strength, and dedication.

An important prerequisite is that you are physically and emotionally healthy enough to make such a fundamental change in your life. If you are currently experiencing a life crisis, it's best to consult with a professional whether such a program is appropriate for you now. This book and its program are not a substitute for therapy. The responsibility for your well-being and your results lies solely with you.

I have developed this book and the 90-Day Program to the best of my knowledge and belief. The contents are based on my personal experiences as a coach and books and lectures by other people. I never studied psychology at university — but I have studied it with many of my fellow human beings and coaches. And I am a startup entrepreneur, father, spouse, and coach by passion.

Always take loving care of you!

Johannes: From management consultant to delivery cook

Three examples to inspire you

To begin our journey, I'd like to share three true stories of people who may have stood in a very similar place in their lives to where you are now. These folks have already made the change you are striving for in a similar way.

More importantly, they, too, have faced fears and obstacles and now openly share how they've overcome them.

One thing is certain: You are not alone in your desire for change.

From investment banker to organic vintner

Achim was spoiled by success. It was more by chance that he ended up in investment banking after his studies and had been earning an increasingly substantial amount of money for a decade. He had not intended to work in this industry for long, but year after year went by without him taking the leap.

In 2015, he realized that without a clear plan, he would never get out. He decided to work for another three years, but at the same time, began to prepare for his departure. When Achim finally handed in his resignation and enjoyed the new peace and quiet at home, he suddenly became ill.

For over a year, he was tormented by the strangest symptoms, and the doctor diagnosed burnout. He learned that overworked people often only get sick when they take a break because as long as there is pressure to perform, the body fires on all cylinders; there is no room for burnout. But as soon as calm finally sets in (often during a long holiday or during the Christmas season), the body *finally* allows itself to slacken off and forces the person to take a break and recover.

Achim was desperate and wondered how he could ever work "normally" again. He thought about what he had enjoyed and what had driven him in the past. Achim came from a farming family and remembered how happy he was working with his parents in the fields and interacting with animals. It was such a contrast to a life mainly about money, shares, returns, meetings, business trips, and status. Achim wasn't into luxury cars or extravagant holidays but preferred to be out in nature alone or with his family. Could he perhaps earn his money that way? Maybe as a tour guide? Or as a farmer?

Achim decided to talk to his wife about it and crunch some numbers to calculate how much money he actually had to earn to lead a decent life. They realized together: Their combined future salary would be more than halved, but since they had put aside a big share of their income anyway, they could live with that much less.

One of his retired friends ran a small organic vineyard, and Achim had always enjoyed helping him with it on weekends. This is how he came up with the idea of doing an internship with a winegrower. The organic winemaker recommended that he go to a larger winegrower and do an apprenticeship.

Achim decided to embark on this adventure. He completed his apprenticeship after two years and now works part-time with the organic winemaker. Achim works half a day, enjoying living with the rhythm of nature. This schedule allows him to volunteer as a consultant to an organization that cares for children in developing countries.

How satisfied is he?

"It was the best decision of my life. It was, of course, an advantage that I was initially in investment banking because that gave me the financial cushion I needed. But looking back, even without such a financial cushion, I would follow my heart and do a job that would give me enough time to live."

People change jobs for two reasons: Pressure from suffering or pressure to change. With Achim, it was the pressure of suffering.

Pressure from suffering arises when your situation burdens you so much over a long period that you urgently want to change the situation. This pressure arises from your work environment where there may be bullying, micromanagement, work that doesn't match your skills, unclear requirements, or unrealistic performance expectations, etc.

Pressure to change arises when you feel the desire to do something new, even though there is nothing fundamental to complain about in your work situation. People are satisfied with their work but want to try something new after many years. Sometimes a job is no longer a good fit because of major life changes like becoming parents or entering a new phase of life. The pressure to change usually drives homemakers back to work again after a few years.

From management to consultant to delivery cook

Johannes was about to take the biggest career step of his life. For ten years — only interrupted by parental leave — he had been working for renowned management consultancies and was on the verge of becoming a partner, i.e., acquiring shares in the company.

He had already worked very hard and knew that his job was about to become much more intense when he became a partner. But wasn't that the whole point of working so hard in the first place?

Right before it happened, Johannes had insomnia; he was doubled over with unexplainable stomach pains and just felt miserable. He kept trying to manage his workload, but at some point, his body let him down.

One morning as he was making breakfast, he had a nervous breakdown. Johannes was taken to the hospital, where the doctor forced him to take a six-month break.

He rested, learned relaxation techniques, did a lot of sports, and was determined to achieve his long-awaited goal of becoming a partner. When he returned to work, he clearly felt that the leadership had already written him off and that he would have to double-down on efforts to become a partner.

Dejected and frustrated, Johannes spoke to a friend about his situation. Shortly after that, Johannes took a long walk in the woods, unable to shake off something his friend said: "Do you really want to stay there for the rest of your life? You have so many talents; why not do something new after ten years?"

Johannes began having doubts about becoming a partner. Wasn't he already dissatisfied with the constant pressure and with the little time he had for himself, his daughter, and his wife? Johannes had already missed so many milestones and precious time with his daughter from age three to seven because he often came home from work when his daughter was already asleep.

He thought about what actually motivated him and his untapped strengths. Johannes loved interacting with people, loved to cook, and was passionate about environmental protection and sustainability. He considered something around ecological gastronomy.

However, the working hours were not feasible. Making a real change meant spending more time with his family.

But how could he work from home (i.e., cook) and still be in contact with his customers? One day he was out for a jog when he came up with a brilliant idea: Prepare dishes at home, package them, and deliver them to customers around his city. He would take orders via the Internet and by phone and then deliver meals to customers in person.

With new-found motivation, he set out to cook three different dishes with regional ingredients from the market as a first test. His first delivery was on a Monday to a company that didn't have their own cafeteria. The friendly staff loved his food and asked for more.

Johannes took his remaining leave from work and extended the test to three other companies. He initially limited deliveries to one day a week so that customers were hungry again for his lovingly prepared dishes. He used the other days for shopping, cooking, and himself and his family.

Satisfaction and demand among the test customers were great. Still, Johannes quickly recognized two problems: If he only sold individual dishes to customers, the cost per dish, including delivery, was too high. The dishes also had to be preserved for several days so that one delivery per week was sufficient.

To solve these problems, he simply put the hot food into Mason jars and set the minimum order quantity at five dishes. The Mason jars were reusable, which met his need for sustainability. In addition, the customers naturally wanted to return the deposit-paid jars, which was easiest if they reordered from him. The concept also proved practical for the customers, as the jars could be conveniently heated in the microwave or double boiler so that all you needed for a delicious meal was a spoon. His selection of exquisite dishes soon became very popular in smaller offices and companies. One of the nicest comments for him was: "It tastes like love filled in glasses."

Johannes has been running his clever delivery service for more than two years. Has he ever regretted this step? I am a loyal customer myself, and when I asked him this question, he replied:

"No, absolutely not! I enjoy cooking, I don't have to run around all day in a suit and tie, I'm at home when my daughter comes home from school, and I can talk to my customers a little, like I'm talking to you right now. I earn considerably less, but it's definitely worth it — my quality of life is much, much higher today."

His story shows how extremely high demands on one's performance and the resulting overwork lead to suffering. A deep health and emotional life crisis arose from this. But his example also shows a crisis always represents an opportunity: the chance to finally tackle a long-standing but suppressed change. In difficult times, you find yourself. Do not avoid them but learn from them.

From law firm to daycare

Martina was frustrated. She was a lawyer and ran a small law firm for social law in a hotspot area of Berlin. She had set up the firm on her own six years ago, and business was going well. Nevertheless, Martina was dissatisfied and kept questioning her life: Why had she actually become a lawyer? She had always loved creative tasks and liked trying out new things. Did she *really* want to continue this job until the end of her working life? Had she perhaps only become a lawyer because her father was a judge and had made her do it consciously or subconsciously?

In fact, she had it all: a secure job, a good income, a man who loved her, and their first child was on the way. You don't just throw away a position that you've worked so hard to build! And didn't she also have an obligation to her clients? What would her friends and family say if, at the age of 40, she threw everything away and started something completely new?

So, for the time being, Martina accepted that work is work. After a short parental leave, she returned to work and continued to bite the bullet. Her daughter attended daycare early, grew up, and soon Martina was expecting a second baby. Far into her pregnancy, she became seriously ill and had to take strong medication. To her great relief, she gave birth to a healthy boy. Martina and her husband enjoyed being parents and did not want to go back to office life. She traced what was really important in her life, and one thing was clear: It wasn't money and status. What was important was family, time, nature, children, and independence.

When the question of childcare arose again, this time for her second child, she and her husband thought that they could simply open a daycare center themselves. Then they would no longer have to hunt down scarce quality daycare centers and could also spend more time with their own children. It was a difficult decision, but it was made quickly. Martina looked for a successor for her office, and only nine months later, they had fulfilled their new dream and opened a daycare in the same building where they lived. Although they now had noticeably less money, Martina had much more time for herself and her family and was happier and more relaxed. Little by little, she grew more and more into the daycare manager's role and enjoyed taking care of the staff and the organization.

Today, she is proud to see how the children enjoy her nursery. This year, 2020, she and her husband — now with a third child — are opening their fourth daycare center and employ over 20 staff members responsible for 80 children.

Martina now feels she is doing the right thing. She is with people, helps children, parents, and their employees, and she can leverage her creativity and craftsmanship when planning and designing the daycare centers. Currently, the two are working on their first children's book in their own publishing house.

Would she do it all over again?

"Yes, definitely! But next time, I wouldn't wait so long to listen to my feelings. I have never missed my lawyer's job since then, and in retrospect, it seems easy to me, which seemed so difficult and risky just a few years ago."

Martina's story is a good example of pressure to change: She could certainly have continued working as a lawyer for a few more years, as she was neither overburdened nor fatally unhappy. But when she experienced the liveliness and joy of being with her children, she sensed there could be so much more to her life.

If you are under pressure to change, you may need such a trigger in your life. Typical examples of other profound life changes include new or terminated relationships, workplace changes, promotions, an intense holiday trip, an accident, deaths, etc.

Right now, you are holding this book in your hands. Has there been a trigger like this in your life lately that you would like to use now? Are you a mother or father of children who are slowly growing up enough so that you can start working again?

To be self-employed means to reveal yourself

"When you notice that you are going in circles, it is time to step out of line!"
~ Author unknown

You will have good reasons for wanting to set up your own business, whether it's due to suffering or pressure to change.

The path to independence means recognizing the dissonance between your expectations and your current reality in life. That way, you can transfer the energy you've been expending on keeping up your façade and direct it toward change. This also means revealing "weakness," and for that, you need courage and strength.

You'll likely encounter naysayers in your circle who will critically question your idea of self-employment. "Don't do something like that; you have a secure job!" "Your partner earns enough; don't you prefer to be at home for the children?" "That's way too risky!" "You have invested so much; you can't throw it all away!"

These are the voices of the social norm, the same voices you may have already heard in your own head. Once you have found the courage to stop listening to your inner voices, you will be equipped to tackle the voices from the outside.

Adverse reactions from others arise from fear. After all, you are rocking the boat and shaking up previous norms. Some of your friends and colleagues may feel the same dissatisfaction but do not have the courage to take such a step themselves. It's easier to badmouth your decision than to question themselves. I hope that you have at least one person in your corner who will be there to support you throughout your journey.

"He who jumps into the unknown owes no explanation to those who watch."
~ JEAN-LUC GODARD, French-Swiss director

In the beginning, deliberately avoid the naggers and doubters; they will only make you insecure and pull you down since you are just taking the first brave steps. But those same naggers and doubters will be valuable later when you've gained enough self-confidence and evolved in yourself and your business idea. Critical feedback helps find and eliminate remaining weak points. Use the critics to test yourself, your business idea, and your arguments. And later in the 90-Day Program, you'll have the best arguments at hand: feedback from real customers who want to buy what you offer.

However, you must have buy-in from those in your domestic environment, especially your spouse/partner and children. Even if they have doubts and would never do it themselves, they should be willing to stand by your commitment to this process. An open and honest agreement with your life partner is imperative. Explain to them how the 90-Day Program works and that it's designed to start your own business with minimal time, cost, and risk as possible, and that a major commitment is only necessary once the business idea has already proven to work.

Your calling will not be silenced

"The only way to be truly fulfilled is to love what you do. If you haven't found that yet, keep looking. For as with all affairs of the heart, you will know when you have found it."[3]
~ STEVE JOBS, co-founder and longtime CEO of Apple, 1955-2011

I am convinced: Every one of us has a unique calling. There is an inner voice guiding you to a specific life vocation. Some even say the world needs something that only you can give it.

When you suppress this calling, you create pain because your inner being is always challenging you to realize your full and true potential. Our authentic self doesn't want to be written off in exchange for acceptance and conformity to the end of our life.

The more a person ignores their true calling, the more likely they are to suffer serious consequences:

- Their work-life has become an unfulfilling, restricted, and passionless existence where they are merely functioning day after day.

- At some point, they numb the pain with addiction (work, alcohol, medicines, drugs, gambling, food, sports, status symbols, etc.)

- ● The body develops a chronic condition that worsens (blood pressure, diabetes, depression, rheumatism, etc.) until the person either comes to his senses (collapse, burnout, etc.) or, in the worst case, dies (e.g., heart attack, stroke).

Of course, I am not claiming that all diseases result from a way of life contrary to one's calling. But I am convinced that in many cases, a "misaligned life" is the psychosomatic trigger of suffering.

Most people believe that the only way their calling will announce itself is during a moment of spontaneity, like an epiphany. They fear that this inspiration may not come, so they just keep waiting for it.

That may happen only in the rarest of cases. As a rule, you only recognize your true calling when you're already in the middle of it. You feel that it simply fits. You feel it in the joy of work, flow, good results, and positive feedback from others when they say, "I can tell how much you love your work."

You will hardly find your true calling if you stay in your old rut and wait for it to hit you over the head. You have to become active, try things out, make mistakes, start over, take risks, do crazy things until, at some point, you realize: "Hmm, I like that. I'm staying here for the time being."

Successfully conforming to a sick society is not a sign of health.

The author Roman Krznaric[4] has compared finding your dream job with dating: You don't usually find your partner by thinking about it and reading books. You have to go out, meet people, fall in love, experience joy and suffering, be left, and leave. At some point, you stay with your partner for life. The work that aligns with your calling is waiting for you somewhere out there, to be discovered or invented.

But what actually constitutes a fulfilled life?

Should one be satisfied with the fact that work is mainly for earning money?

Is it realistic to expect personal fulfillment, satisfaction, or even happiness from one's job?

In my opinion, this expectation is less realistic if one has a full-time position in a big corporation (even if some of them may actually succeed). But if you are self-employed, you can absolutely expect this!

Being rich is not about who has much, but who needs little

That brings us to a fundamental question about your independence: What do you really need for a happy life? What makes your life rich? What does your inner voice tell you? And what role does the money earned through gainful employment play for you?

The 90-Day Program defines "rich" as:[5]

- **Time** to do the things that make you happy with

- **People** who enrich you.

- **Independence** to make your own decisions.

- **Income** to support your lifestyle.

The actual value of your income, therefore, depends on the four "W" questions, which you are free to answer:

1. *What* do you do?

2. *When* do you do it?

3. *Where* do you do it?

4. With *whom* do you do it?

Imagine that you have a high income, but due to your job, you have neither the time nor the independence to answer the above "W" questions about your wellbeing. This is true for many people we consider "successful."

Take business meals as an example. These can be enjoyable experiences, or simply, an unpleasant duty. Imagine, for instance, that you have a well-paid management position in sales at an international company. You might eat at the best restaurants and drink exquisite wines, but with people you may not like. You're forced to be good-humored even though you are under pressure to achieve a business goal, only to come home late when your partner and children are already asleep. Here, you don't have control over the four "W" questions because your job dictates them.

Now compare this with a life where you are self-employed with less responsibility and an average income, where you schedule your time. While the salesperson "enjoys" the business dinner described above, you might be sitting on a park bench with your partner on a balmy summer evening, eating a fresh baguette with a glass of red wine, and having a relaxed conversation. Or you can play with your children in the autumn forest, throwing leaves at each other and tickling them until they squeal with laughter and then enjoy a hot cocoa.

Who do you feel is "richer?" And what will you think back to when you reach the end of your life – the business dinner or the time with your loved ones? And what will your children think? They will undoubtedly want more mom and dad rather than more house or more stuff.

As Brené Brown[6] put it: "*We chase after extraordinary moments instead of being grateful for the ordinary ones. And then in the face of really hard times — illness, death, loss — we beg to relive the ordinary moments.*"

The Covid-19 era was (and still is) a time of great challenge. For example, both working parents have to balance work responsibilities virtually while providing home study and childcare. Now double that stress for single parents. At the same time, many people have experienced how good it feels without the hustle and bustle to have more time for themselves, their family, the house and/or garden, exploring nature, and taking long walks and bike rides. Restricted shopping and travel have reduced the struggle with existential hardships, returning people to what really counts in their lives.

Money is important. But more income only makes you happier up to a certain point, and that point is reached sooner than many people think (between $60,000 and $120,000 per year, depending on the study).[7] After that, the problems tend to increase with income. Pythagoras is said to have coined the following fitting aphorism: "*Rich in money means poor in pleasures.*"

One of the 90-Day Program's tasks will ask you to determine the personal income you need to be satisfied.

Here is an excellent illustration (which may sound familiar) of happiness versus wealth:[8]

An investment banker urgently needed a holiday and is recovering in a small Mexican coastal village when a fisherman's small boat moors. Several large, fresh fish lay in the boat.

The investment banker is impressed by the quality of the fish and asks the Mexican how long it took him to catch them. The Mexican replies, "Just a little while." The banker then asks why he didn't stay out longer to catch more fish.

The Mexican fisherman replies that he has enough to feed his family. The investment banker replies, "But what do you do with the rest of your time?"

The fisherman replies, "I sleep late, fish a little, play with my children, take siestas with my wife, stroll every evening to the village where I drink wine, and play the guitar with my amigos. I have a full and busy life, señor."

The investment banker mocks, "I come from the best business school in the world and could help you. You could spend more time fishing and use the proceeds to buy a bigger boat, and with the proceeds from the bigger boat, you could buy several boats until you finally have a whole fleet of fishing boats. Instead of selling your catch to the middleman, you could sell it directly to the processor and eventually open your own cannery. You could control the product, processing, and distribution." Then he adds, "Of course, you would have to leave this small fishing village on the coast and move to Mexico City, where you would run your growing business."

The Mexican asks, "But, señor, how long will all this take?"

To which the banker replies, "Fifteen to 20 years."

"But then what?" the Mexican asks.

The investment banker laughs and says, "This is the best part. When the time is right, you would announce an IPO, sell your shares, and become very rich. You could make millions!"

"Millions, señor? And then what?"

The investment banker replies: "Then you could retire. You could move to a small fishing village on the coast, where you could sleep in, do some fishing, play with your children, have a siesta with your wife, go for a walk in the evening to the village where you could drink wine and play guitar with your amigos..."

Living a happy life is actually quite simple: Do the things that are good for you and leave out the things that are not good for you. Done. It's simple, isn't it? But then why do we often act like the investment banker and not like the fisherman?

I believe "courage" is key to answering this question.

About courage, decisions, and consequences

"Beginning comes before skill."
~ Author unknown

When I talk to people who are dissatisfied with their lives and want to change something but can't, I usually hear one of the following reasons:

- ✖ I don't know exactly what I want. (= missing target)

- ✖ I don't know how. (= lack of knowledge about the way)

- ✖ I can't do it. (= lack of ability or lack of means)

- ✖ I can't make it. (= lack of discipline)

- ✖ One cannot merely … (= self-limitation through standards)

- ✖ I do not dare … (= lack of courage)

I've heard so often that someone in an unsatisfactory job simply doesn't know what they want to do. But when I ask a few questions, I quickly reach a point where these people start out a bit shy and sometimes ashamed at first, but then, with a sparkle in their eyes, their entire body language changes and suddenly they are animated when they talk about their longstanding dreams. And these dreams are often already very concrete, and as an outsider, seem anything but unrealistic. However, this is quite absurd for the person because censors from childhood are raising the usual red flags, saying, "You can't do that! No, you just can't do that!"

I am convinced that most people with all the above concerns only lack one characteristic …

COURAGE!

A little more critically, one could also say, it's about comfort. "The situation I'm in is very uncomfortable, but it's more comfortable (i.e., it demands less of me) to just stay in the situation, endure it, and relieve the dissatisfaction by whining."

Have you ever noticed that people who display courage are admired by everyone, even if they don't achieve anything "great?" For example, the courage to have an opinion against resistance, the courage to say, "I love you" first, the courage to talk about your illness, the courage to say "no," etc. This is because such courage is quite rare.

Your path to independence inevitably means that in the future, you will no longer adhere to many "norms" you've given yourself along the way. That seems threatening at first because it means that you're stepping out of your present way of life. You will contradict the expectations and ideas of society, your friends, and/or your parents. You will then be someone different than before!

How will it feel? What kind of person are you then? That is new and uncertain, a risk you have shied away from for years. That's why this step takes so much courage. That's why you are so afraid of it and tell yourself things like: "I just can't do it." "I will not be successful," or "I don't know if I really want it; in fact, I don't know what I want at all."

But remember: With courage, you pay the price *beforehand* and reap your reward later. With adaptation, the *reward* comes *first* (e.g., you join in and submit, get a pat on the back!), and you pay the price later (painful dissatisfaction with yourself and your conformed life).

Unfortunately, there is no way around it. You must summon up the courage to take the step into the unfounded fear.

Perhaps it will help you if you imagine your fear as a seemingly insurmountable obstacle that you have to overcome to get ahead. Unfortunately, you neither know what it looks like on the other side, nor can you simply go back once you have surpassed it.

Fear is a natural reaction to moving closer to the truth.

Are fear and trepidation desirable? Of course not! But you can count on the following:

Once you have overcome your fear — it no longer feels threatening at all. In hindsight, you'll think: "That wasn't so bad after all!" It turns out that this overwhelming feeling of impending doom was just lukewarm air, triggering fear of the unknown that built up so menacingly in your head. You will be surprised when people suddenly tell you how brave you are. At that point, you feel more at ease, and, most importantly, you'll rediscover yourself. Once you've reached that point, you'll never dream of wanting to go back to where you are today.

The observation of business angel Fabian Hansmann: *"I have never met a founder who regrets having founded a company"* aligns with my experience. Entrepreneurs overcome fear with courage and do not want to go back afterward. Even if their company was not financially successful, they were successful as founders by daring to try something new and learning and growing through their experience.

I started my first company back in 2008 — a carpooling portal on the Internet — and it was a financial flop. Nevertheless, I was glad to have tried it and proud of what my co-founder and I had achieved. Even though we couldn't make a living from this first business, we did advance the carpooling market (our ideas were adopted by established providers and are standard today). Prospective employers recognized and were impressed by my courage to start my own business. By the way, our second startup in 2009 was successful, and only one year later, we successfully sold our company, miniPay (today www.sepa.net), to a strategic investor.

Action cures fear. And behind it lie all your possibilities.

To reach your goal, be prepared to courageously contradict societal expectations — as well as the ones in your head and the expectations bestowed upon you by others: "You say *that's* how it's done? But I do it *this* way." And: "You say *you* don't do that? But *I* do it anyway because I do it for me and not for you (anymore)."

In the 90-Day Program, you'll complete various exercises to learn how to: leave your comfort zone, develop courage and its physical manifestation in your posture, stand by yourself, and go your own way. Because if you know why you're doing something, you have the courage to do it.

Viktor Frankl put it in a nutshell:

> *"Those who know the 'why' they live for can endure almost any 'how.'"*
> ~ Viktor Frankl, Austrian neurologist and psychiatrist, author and Holocaust survivor, 1905-1997

Of course, decisions can be bold yet wrong. So how can courage be distinguished from overconfidence?

For example, it would be overconfident to take your entire savings to the casino and bet it all on red in roulette. This can go well, and your money can double from one moment to the next. Or you can lose it just as irretrievably and end up in a financial disaster.

It depends on whether a decision can have existentially threatening consequences or not. Therefore, it is necessary to examine: Is your decision putting everything irrevocably at risk? Or, are possible negative consequences correctable in the medium and long term? Could you live with the consequences?

For example, if you decide to quit your job and it turns out to be a mistake, you can find a new job. If you are a stay-at-home parent and decide to go back to work, and it doesn't work out, you can quit your job and return to fulltime parenting. Such consequences are not the end of the world, even if the thought of it often feels that way at first.

> *"In the moments you make decisions, you shape your destiny."*
> ~ Tony Robbins, U.S. author, and coach trainer

But how do I know whether a decision is right or wrong?

There is no clear answer to this very understandable question for at least two reasons:

1. It depends on *when* you answer the question. After ten minutes, after ten weeks, or after ten years? A supposedly bad decision may turn out to be surprisingly good later on or, conversely, that a seemingly good decision will turn out to be a great misfortune later on because of unexpected consequences.

2. You can never know how your life and the world would have turned out by a decision *not made*. So, you can never say for sure that you would have really been better or worse with the alternative.

The only thing you can do is make any decision to the best of your ability and then let time pass. Only in time can you determine what is happening and correct the course if necessary.

Incidentally, *to decide to do nothing* is not the same thing as *not to decide at all*. Deciding to do nothing (for the time being) can sometimes be very sensible and the best decision. It allows new possibilities to emerge over time, which you can then consciously choose to do.

What works for me is using my inner voice as a decision-making aid. If I've wanted to do something for a long time or the thought frequently recurs, but I just don't dare, then I am convinced I should do it! As soon as I become aware of it, I try to overcome my discomfort and just do it.

Try it out for yourself! It starts with the person you don't dare talk to, the course you've always wanted to take, or the job you've always wanted to do, the one that doesn't match your parents' expectations or your present career. The 90-Day Program will provide distinct tasks to help you consciously move out of your comfort zone.

The important thing is to *not* condemn or punish yourself just because you think you've made the wrong decision. Such decisions may require correction or new solutions, but rarely punishment. There is no success without error, sacrifice, or renunciation. And always: Who knows how it might benefit you in the future?

Remember the lawyer, investment banker, and management consultant from Chapter 1, who are now a daycare teacher, an organic winegrower, and a delivery cook? All of them brooded for months or years over the decision, sweating blood before they summoned all their courage to make such a significant change. But they did it, and of course, there were moments when it felt like a bad decision. Moments when they wished they could have gone back to the "other side" and escaped into their old life.

But such crises passed, and they found new ways that they wouldn't have imagined before. And — as things stand today — they are happy to live so self-determinedly and independently. Is it certain that it will always stay that way? Of course not! They may think in three, five, or ten years: If only I had done something else! But then maybe there will simply be a time in life when a bigger decision will have to be made.

When's the right time?

"The best time to plant a tree was 20 years ago. The second best is now."
~ Chinese proverb

When is the right time to live the dream of independence? The time is never "right!" There are always "good" reasons why it's not the right time right now: "I don't have enough money to dare do this!" "Not until the children are out of the house!" "I first have to solve my problems with my current job!" "Maybe when I have a partner!" "If I didn't have a partner!" and so on.

The right time never *comes*; the right time is ***now***! After all, today is the beginning of the rest of your life!

And if you read this book in 2020 or 2021, those times are indeed ideal, because times of crisis are the perfect moment to build something new, as I explained earlier.

If not now, then when?

The six steps of the 90-Day Program

Step by step to successful independence

"Nobody knows what he can do until he tries."
~ Publilius Syrus, Roman author in the 1st century BC

Here, I will first provide a short overview of the six steps that you will master one at a time in the program. These will be developed in subsequent chapters.

We start with your **motivation** and your **strengths**. Then you will learn how to **free up time** because the time required for the tasks steadily increases. You will systematically develop your **business idea** and test it on real customers as soon as possible. During this process, you will only concentrate on the **things you really have to (or want to) do.** I will introduce you to competent **service companies** for the rest. Finally, there is the question of **how big you should make your business** so that you don't miss your "point of sufficiency," but remain satisfied with your independence in the long run.

IMPORTANT: Start with task no. 1 now!

If you haven't done it yet, start your 90-Day Program now. Our motto is: Less theory, more action! That means start the program, do your homework every day, **and** continue reading this book.

You can easily complete the first two weeks of tasks without reading the book, so there's no reason to wait: Choose the day to start your 90-Day Program — it could be today — and follow the instructions on page 99.

So, have you set your start date?

If so, you can now find out what to expect in the 90-Day Program.

If not, read on now, but plan your start date first.

---

1. Recognize your motivation and strengths

Your path to success is driven by *why* you want to become self-employed in the first place. What are your expectations? What problems do you want to solve today? Is it about more freedom and flexibility? If so, what do you want to use it for? For your children, your hobbies, for other people? Or is it about self-fulfillment, about creating something that you've been dreaming about for a long time? Or are you hoping for more money? What would you do with the money?

So, the question is, what exactly motivates you to be self-employed? Think about this carefully because your answer will give you the strength to go the distance and will be why you get out of bed in the morning. While willpower, stamina, and discipline are the necessary building blocks for achieving your goal, your **internal motivation** is the foundation that strengthens and binds them. Without it, reaching your goal will be difficult at best.

Therefore, the first two weeks focuses on your motivation and strengths. You won't need much time for these tasks yet. However, as it becomes more time-consuming from the third week on, you'll learn in the second step how to buy the time you need.

2. Create time for your business idea

If you're employed or have children at home, this is perhaps your biggest question: With all this stress, how am I supposed to find *additional* time to build up my independence?

Don't worry; it *will* work. The 90-Day Program provides tasks for practical techniques that will help you in all areas of your life to have more time for things you value.

This is about becoming more effective in your current work and everyday life. It's not just about *how* you do things, but you'll also determine what you're going to completely *stop* doing.

We take a hard look at those things you can "sacrifice" in your private life to work on your independence with a clear conscience. I'm talking about things like watching television, surfing the Internet, or playing around on your phone. You *should not* reduce the time you spend with your loved ones or with your hobbies. Our aim is to have *more* time for that. After all, we don't want to wait until the future to live life.

To free up time, the 90-Day Program will give you a chance to look at your current working methods, learn key principles for effectiveness, and set the right priorities. It's about working smarter, which means you should have more time *and* better results than before.

3. Discover your business idea

After the basic idea for your self-employment has taken shape (What you want to do) based on your motivation and your strengths, you will define the different aspects of your self-employment in the 90-Day Program (How you want to work). That includes questions such as when, where, and how much you want to work, how much income you need, and with, and for whom you work, etc.

Here I will introduce you to different business models and case studies of successful founders from which you can draw inspiration for your personal calling.

4. Develop and test your business idea

We are working under the assumption that you have little time and not much money to start your own business and need to minimize financial risk. Therefore, it is key to budget your time as efficiently as possible throughout the entire 90-Day Program.

That is why, with minimal effort, as early as possible, you will test the viability of your idea on real customers: Are there enough customers willing to buy your product or service for the price you determine? This essential information must come quickly so that you can adapt your idea to viability before you run out of breath, time, and/or money.

Testing early means that you try to sell your offer even though it is not yet ready. Because if it doesn't find any buyers, you're glad you didn't finish it in the first place. And if customers want to buy it, you can be sure that your offer is now worth the effort.

There are clever methods for this type of testing, which you will learn and apply in the 90-Day Program. In this way, you'll not only get a better feeling for whether your idea will be successful, but you'll also get to know your market and your customers better and better.

5. Do only what you like and outsource the rest

To successfully implement a business idea with little time and money — perhaps even in the long term for part-time work — the 90-Day Program directs you to concentrate on those activities that only you *can* do or that you *would like to* do.

You can safely delegate all other tasks to service companies. Today, this is much easier and cheaper than you might think. For example, did you know that there are companies on the Internet that manage your phone calls for just a few dollars a month? Or design agencies that create logos, business cards, or flyers for you for $30?

Everything you need is available today with just a few clicks and can be canceled monthly. That saves a lot of time and money, and you remain financially flexible. The 90-Day Program will guide you step-by-step to find suitable partners for individual areas of responsibility.

6. Determine your perfect scale of your business

During the 90 days, you will test and develop your business idea until you have the confidence to flip the switch and make your business idea a reality with increased effort and investment. If you are employed, you can then — if you wish — say goodbye to your old job and submit your resignation. Because now, the growth phase begins. But how big do you actually want to grow your business idea?

One task in the 90-Day Program is to calculate the minimum and maximum amount of money you need to live. Did I say maximum? Yes. That is a rare question in our society, as it is usually about making as much money as possible.

Since more money tends to weigh more heavily at a certain point, the 90-Day Program is also about finding the right balance for your lifestyle so that you don't end up in a new hamster wheel out of enthusiasm for growth.

"I can do it!"

Step 1:
Identify your motivation and strengths

"If you want to be happy for a day, get drunk.
If you want to be happy for a year, get married.
If you want to be happy for life, be a gardener."
~ Chinese proverb

What is your motivation?

Many books on self-employment or business start-ups consider getting rich as quickly as possible as the primary motivation, such as *How to Get Rich* (Dennis Felix), *The Laptop Millionaire* (Mark Anastasi), or *The Millionaire Fastlane* (MJ DeMarco). Maybe this works for some people to some degree. But do they promise you to be satisfied or even happy?

My goal for you is long-term fulfillment and a healthy balance in your new job, rich in time and freedom, not necessarily excessively rich in money. So, if you're convinced that the road to happiness is to get rich quickly, then choose one of the other books.

But before you do, please consider the top five regrets of people on their deathbeds:[9]

- ✔ I wish I had had the courage to live my own life.

- ✔ I wish I had not worked so much.

- ✔ I wish I had had the courage to express my feelings.

- ✔ I wish I had maintained contact with my friends.

- ✔ I wish I had allowed myself to be happier.

None of the dying wished they had earned more money, worked more, or bought more. Your perspective sharpens and simplifies as you realize what really matters because there is no time to change things in the face of death.

According to one of the most common psychological theories,[10] people strive to satisfy three basic needs: Attachment to other people, autonomy, and competency or self-efficacy.

Here it is clear what an important role our work plays in our lives. Since our job can satisfy (or not satisfy) all three needs, it follows that we invest a large part of our life and time in our work.

According to this theory, the nightmare job would thus be an activity in which one works in isolation (no attachment to other people) and under strict guidelines (no autonomy) without seeing the fruits of one's labor (no experience of competence or self-efficacy).

On the other hand, a dream job would involve surrounding yourself with like-minded, talented people, leveraging your strengths in a self-determined way, and experiencing the benefits of your work.

Now that we've wrapped our heads around theory, let's dive into reality. The extent to which these three needs are prominent in your professional life depends on your personality and ability to satisfy these needs in your private life.

In addition to these general basic human needs, you have individual talents and gifts and a resulting vocation for the world. And it is your task to hear this call and pursue it.

If you follow this call and do what you love, you will make yourself and others happy. And you are an example for others to listen to their heart as well.

Knowing that you want to leave your current situation is not enough. You need to know what you *really* want instead, *where* you want to go, and *what* your goal is.

Right now, this is your chance to do what makes you happy, regardless of what others think about it.

Is it perhaps a "crazy" idea? Great! That is a good sign that you're on the right track, because if it's not "crazy," it's "normal," i.e., it follows standard expectations and does not break new ground. Others are already doing it, and there will be more competitors.

What you want deep down inside is also called **intrinsic motivation**, which results in pleasure and well-being. In contrast, **extrinsic motivation** is when you do something only because you receive an external reward, like money, recognition, or security.

Most workers are extrinsically motivated because they'd never perform their job without pay. The 90-Day Program is about discovering your intrinsic motivation to determine the type of work you enjoy while earning enough to sustain your lifestyle.

During the first two weeks, you will therefore examine your motivation from various angles:

- **What did you want to be when you grew up?** As children, our intuition was on-point because we had yet to be strongly influenced by social norms. However, family influence is powerful, which means that it's important to also deal with your parents' expectations.

- **What have been incredibly beautiful experiences in your life?** Maybe you did something on holiday that was exceptionally good for you. Perhaps you had an internship or a job in the past that felt "right."

- **Who are your role models?** Are there people who have always fascinated you? For example, famous personalities or people from your environment, such as grandparents, parents, siblings, friends, or colleagues? What distinguishes these people? What have they done differently from others around you? What values do they represent, and what do they embody for you?

- **Which tasks are particularly easy for you?** In my experience, this is one of the best indicators of what you're "made for." Surprisingly, we often don't recognize these qualities in ourselves because they come naturally and are "not a big deal." The 90-Day Program will unearth your unique attributes by having you ask about them from trusted people in your social and professional circle.

- **What would you do if you didn't have to earn money?** Imagine receiving an unconditional basic income that would sustain your lifestyle. What would you do then? How would you spend your days? If you leave out the compulsion to earn money, it's easier to think about what you would actually like to do.

Apart from clarifying what really motivates you, it's also essential to discover your strengths and skills and how you can leverage them for your business idea.

Discovering and developing your calling

People often expect a magical moment will suddenly reveal their calling, and then end up waiting for a moment that will never happen. Some also feel insecure when asked during a conversation what their calling is and feel stupid for not being able to answer at their advanced age.

I would like to briefly unravel some myths about one's "calling:"

- **One day, your calling will fall into your lap.** Good luck with that. Often, you only recognize your calling once you've already lived it — at least in part. Voluntarily or involuntarily, you start something new (e.g., you have to take care of a sick person), and after some time, you notice how it invigorates you, how skilled you are at it, and how natural it feels to you. You may have just gotten in touch with your calling (in this example, to be a caretaker).

- **Your calling is something you've already mastered.** Even Mozart had to practice! Natural skills require development, like a baby first learning to walk.[11] When you've discovered your calling, it doesn't mean that you have mastered everything necessary to perform that role. The good news is your learning curve will be enjoyable and relatively short, but you must give it time. That is why the 90-Day Program is so well-suited to employees who don't dare quit their jobs to try self-employment. You can use your "breadwinning" job to gradually develop your calling into your future income.

We take the time for things we value

If you have time to surf the Internet, watch Netflix or television, or play video games, you obviously value those activities enough to carve out time for them.

However, I maintain that the statement, "We only take time for the things that are important to us," even applies to an insufferable job. Why is a job so important to you that you invest a large part of your day, even if you don't like it?

If you like your current job, skip to the next chapter.

If you do not like your current job, prepare to be provoked!

Ready?

I say: **You are where you want to be.**

What? Do I really claim that you *want* to be in this job or this current situation?

Yes, that is exactly what I'm saying!

Now before you throw this book across the room, let me add something else:

You are where you want to be ... because all other options — consciously or subconsciously — have been too "expensive" for you so far.

You don't *have* to do your job, because nobody holds a gun to your head and forces you to do it. But you do it. Probably for the money. Or medical insurance or...

In your head — at least in your subconscious mind — the following thought has probably circulated frequently:

"Oh, I should dump this crap and start something new. Screw them! Hmm, but then I won't earn any money for a while. And what will I do instead? I'll have to job-hunt, apply to a bunch of jobs, go through who knows how many interviews. Then, I'll have to start at the bottom, re-establish myself, and maybe even move and/or have to go through another painful learning curve. Oh my gosh! I'm tired and nervous just thinking about it! I think I'll stay in my stupid job a little longer and think about doing something else later."

What's happening here is that your mind weighs the costs of different options, where "costs" refers not only to money but also to time, effort, uncertainty, learning, etc. So, the claim that you are exactly where you *want* to be is correct: You *could* change it, but that change is too "expensive."

In the 90-Day Program, you'll learn methods to focus on what is truly important and meaningful for you in your private and professional life. You'll also develop the courage and self-confidence to embark on your own path to independence.

How to discover your individual strengths

We all have strengths and weaknesses. Many people are more aware of their weaknesses than their strengths and consequently suffer from a lack of self-esteem. If that sounds familiar, rest assured, you're not alone.

Ideally, your motivation and strengths are already well-matched. However, if you've gone through life suppressing your motivation, chances are you haven't had the opportunity to fully develop the strengths that match your motivation.

Either way, you'll take the strengths you have (you can read this book here, for example) and use them to develop the idea of self-employment that matches your motivation.

Another critical aspect of strengths: Every strength has a so-called "accepted weakness." For example, if you are very creative, generate many ideas, and discover completely novel solutions to problems, you are unlikely to be a proficient and passionate accountant. Because creative people are usually less structured, they think more about possibilities and not within given structures, more about the future than about the past. An accountant, however, is not supposed to invent anything new, but to record the completed payment transactions within a given structure. As a result, a thoroughbred accountant tends to find it rather difficult to develop radically new ideas. Therefore, come to terms with your accepted weaknesses — the opposite of your strengths — and find suitable partners for these tasks.

Key insight: **Focus your time and energy on developing your strengths rather than overcoming your weaknesses.** The progress you can make with your weaknesses is limited and takes a lot of effort and time, whereas working on your strengths is easy and will bring significant progress quickly.

In the first two weeks, you will learn a lot about yourself:

- We will start with the **strengths that you recognize in yourself.** These may be manual skills, special knowledge, a knack for dealing with people, writing and communicating well, or artistic skills. These strengths also include virtues such as perseverance, flexibility, thoroughness, patience, etc.

- **You will ask other people who know you well for their opinion**: "Where do you see my strengths? What have I done particularly well in the past? What are the first qualities that come to your mind when you think of me? On what topics would you ask me for advice?"

- **Which tasks do you perform exceptionally well at work?** On which topics do people ask for your advice? What are you known for at work? (e.g., Are you the "go-to" person for a software program?) What are your job responsibilities, and what do you see as your strengths? What are you often praised for?

- **What did you do particularly well as a child and teenager?** What were your hobbies that you no longer have today (e.g., caring for animals, painting, sports, reading)? What do your parents or grandparents remember when they think of you in your childhood? What did they enjoy doing? How did you like to spend your holidays, and how did you spend your free time? And with whom? Did you prefer to be alone, or did you like having lots of people around you? What did you excel at?

- **What kinds of problems do you like to solve?** What challenges you? What types of tasks do you like to volunteer for? Where have you shone in the past with particularly good solutions?

By exploring your motivation and strengths from different angles, the 90-Day Program helps you paint a comprehensive and realistic picture of yourself and your capabilities. Without this knowledge, you may not have realized your full potential for many years.

Step 1 Side-Effect Warning: You may experience increased self-confidence and self-esteem!

Focus systematically on your goal

Step 2:
Create time for your business idea

"When the time comes when you could, the time is over when you can. "
~ Marie von Ebner-Eschenbach, Moravian-Austrian writer (1830-1916)

The question I am asked most often is: "My plate is already full. Where am I going to find the time to develop a business idea as well?" The 90-Day Program assigns targeted tasks to solve this problem, the basics of which I describe below.

Have you ever noticed that you usually don't finish a task until the last minute, no matter how much time you have? If we have too much time, we typically postpone the task until the pressure is significant enough to finally act (think tax return!). That is also known as Parkinson's Law: *"A task always takes as much time as you give it."*

On the other hand, has everyone experienced that a task for which there is actually far too little time (e.g., because it only comes to mind the day before the deadline) is then particularly well done? That is because the time pressure makes you much more pragmatic. After all, you can't afford any distractions or dead ends, and you only focus on completing the task on time. So, to complete things successfully, you often don't need more time, but a tight deadline: just enough to get the job done just in time.

You have no idea how creative you can get! Of course, you should not use this procedure all the time, because it also means stress. But don't say: "In the next two weeks, I will take care of my company logo," but rather: "Tonight at 8 pm, I will take two hours to develop an idea for a company logo, look at three suppliers and ask for a draft."

The 90-Day Program uses this principle in two ways:

1. It gives you a task for each day, which you will usually complete in full on that day.

2. The whole process is limited to a relatively short period of 90 working days. Classically, it is more likely to take at least six to twelve months to start your own business!

Reach 80% of your results in 20% of your time

It's incredible how much of a task can be accomplished in 20 percent of the total time actually required. And how much time it takes to make it a little better: You would need another 80 percent of your time/energy/money to reach the last 20 percent of the result, but in most cases, this is not necessary at all.

This important principle was developed by the economist Vilfredo Pareto (1848-1923). He found that most tasks can be completed with 20% resource input so that 80% of all problems are solved (also known as the Pareto principle or the 80/20 Rule).

You will learn how to leverage this insight to optimize your time and energy at work and in your private life. The time you gained will be used to create your independence.

Only a few (truly) vital tasks matter

At any given moment, only a small number of tasks are actually urgent and important. That said, your to-do list can be as long as you like, including tasks that are unnecessary *right now or entirely* unnecessary. Why do we engage in work that is not absolutely essential at the moment? Because we crave the satisfying feeling of being "busy."

Think about your work for a moment: If you add up all the time you are really productive in one day — how many hours or minutes do you come up with? On the other hand, how much time do you waste on things that are neither important nor urgent and don't help your company and your customers at all? Reading, answering, and sorting emails, searching for documents, attending meetings for the sake of meeting, reading reports, etc. What is the result at the end of the workday? How often do you think in the evening: Was it worth going to work? Unfortunately, too many days achieve too little. You are partially responsible for this, but much of the lack of productivity is due to your employer's work environment and culture.

You *can* change this. You cannot change your employer, but you can leave them. Suppose you are satisfied with your employment, for now. In that case, the 90-Day Program process focuses on: Optimizing your actions at work and daily life to become more effective in all areas of your life. At the same time, you start developing your business idea. And — if you are unhappily employed — to quit *only* when you determine you are secure enough to be self-employed fulltime.

How to create freedom in daily life

There are opportunities in your personal life to free up time for your business idea. If your home looks like 98% of your fellow human beings, you have a television, a computer, a smartphone, and maybe even a game console.

People in Europe watch between two (Switzerland) and five hours (Romania) of television a day. In Germany, people use the Internet three (over age 14) to six hours a day (between ages 14 to 29). Often, additional time is spent on video games and social media on smartphones.[12] So, chances are, that with a little discipline and completely free of charge, you could free up *two hours a day* in your private life without sacrificing active time with your family or for yourself.

If you want to change your life — and that´s what starting your own business truly is — then this is an excellent time to tackle some other areas that have been bothering you for a long time. Only focus on things that are reasonably easy to change. Other changes will come later (for example, it is very difficult to quit smoking, so it's better to tackle smoking cessation after completing the 90-Day Program).

The program includes tasks that will help you clean up and simplify your life, reduce your media consumption, direct your energy, and focus on yourself and your business idea.

How to create freedom at work

If you are currently employed, use the following means to create the necessary freedom at work:

- ◆ Vacation
- ◆ Sick leave
- ◆ Sabbatical
- ◆ Part-time
- ◆ Home office
- ◆ Use existing free time around work (e.g., commuting distances)
- ◆ Becoming more effective to create new freedom around work

Vacation

The easiest way is to create time and space to work on your business idea is to take a vacation, especially if you have already accumulated enough vacation time, and you don't need it for your family. Often there are other options you should consider, such as educational leave.

Sick leave

Due to excessive workloads and sometimes dysfunctional corporate cultures, more and more people are taking sick leave from work and are then absent for weeks or months at a time. I speak from personal experience. I had burn-out, and it took almost a whole year before I was mentally healthy again. In that case, it takes a significant amount of time before you can get back on your feet. But that time is also often an opportunity to leave the beaten track and find a new direction. This means that even a prolonged illness can be used to start creating your dream job. However, this should always be done under professional supervision by a psychologist or psychiatrist, so that you do not become ill again.

Sabbatical

More and more companies offer their employees the opportunity to take a break for a longer period after a few years of employment. During this time, you don't usually receive a salary, but your job remains secure. This is an excellent way to develop your business idea without risk. If it works, you won't return. And if you're not successful, you can go back to your old job and try again later.

It's important that you obey the employment laws of your country/state. In some countries, you have to obtain your employer's consent for a secondary job. Normally, the employer has no problems with this, as long as it doesn't hurt the employee's work and doesn't result in a competitive situation. Make sure that the self-employment job does not violate any non-competes and does not negatively impact your job performance or attendance.

Part-time

In my experience, a part-time job is an ideal way to implement your own business idea without having to forego a steady income. Although you earn less in part-time employment, you also have regular and predictable time to work on your own business idea. Some people already work part-time, for example, and look after their children. When the need for childcare diminishes, this is an excellent opportunity to develop one's own business idea during part-time work, instead of working full-time in an employed job.

Perhaps you can also negotiate a part-time arrangement with your employer? You will also systematically take care of this in the 90-Day Program, if this is an option for you.

Home office

If your company values hours worked and the perception of "busy-ness" over productivity, you will feel incredibly liberated working in a home office. During the Covid pandemic, many companies and employees involuntarily experienced the advantages and disadvantages of working from home. At home, without all of the distractions of an office environment, you often accomplish more in a few hours than in a whole day at the office. You can use the time saved to work on your idea.

I will show you how to convince your superiors to let you work at home one or more days a week.

Use existing free time

During the program, you will discover free time already built into your workday to use for your business idea. There is much more potential than you think! Right now, envision your workdays from start to finish. There is the journey to work in the car or by public transport, and possibly business trips that can be used. There are waiting or idle times at work, which you might fill up with trivial things like surfing the Internet or chatting with coworkers. Discover idle time around work training courses, especially if they are out of town, and you spend the night away from home.

Creating new freedom

I don't know whether you are currently working in a profession and — if so — how you have organized your working day. When you follow the process, the 90-Day Program will make you much more effective at work because you'll only focus on crucial tasks. You'll use the time you have freed up to develop yourself and for making your dream come true.

What is the difference between *effectiveness* and *efficiency*? Being efficient means doing something *right*, i.e., achieving a specific goal with as few resources as possible. A little more concrete: If you manage to process your daily mountain of 50 emails in one hour instead of two, you are twice as efficient. Sounds good, right?

Not necessarily.

Because if processing emails doesn't bring you closer to your actual work goal, you've been spectacularly efficient, but wildly ineffective.

Being *effective* means doing the *right* things that move you closer to your goal. And suppose your job is to acquire new customers, for example. In that case, it's probably better to call potential customers than to go through countless internal emails that have nothing to do with securing customers.

Unfortunately, many companies do not value output. Instead, they applaud the number of hours one works and how "busy" one appears. This is doubly problematic: First, fewer results are achieved, and second, new employees are trained to be "busy" rather than effective. Enough people spend all day in meetings and rush stressed from one appointment to another, but hardly ever get around to implementing anything and producing concrete results. Before, after, and during meetings, they may then create many emails to a long list of recipients to reinforce the impression that they are "working" a lot. That is how work becomes work theatre.

The trick is to do *much less,* not more, and concentrate only on the activities that will help you and your job (especially those of your employer if you are still employed). During and after the 90-Day Program, you will do a lot more in a lot less time.

Apply the Pareto principle, mentioned above, to analyze your workday more closely. You'll find that 80% of your communication is with 20% of your colleagues. Similarly, 80% of your results are achieved by 20% of your work efforts, which leaves 80% work effort that *marginally* contributes to your results and/or 80% work effort that is noncontributory and unproductive.

So, your goal is to focus on the 20% (input = time, customers, task, products, etc.) that have a direct impact on the 80% (output) and ignore the rest (as long as this doesn't result in critical consequences). You can then allocate the significant time savings to the remaining 20% output or use the extra time for your business idea.

Your increased productivity not only means more time for your idea, but it also strengthens your position to negotiate for more flexibility, working at home, and time off.

In the 90-Day Program, you will be given tasks to systematically free up more time in your professional life and at home, without giving up the people and things that are really important to you.

Work, family, and work-life balance

I think my convictions have now become clear: A lot of money will never make you happy for long, but you need enough of it to live. We value time and the freedom to enjoy it with the people we cherish.

The phrase "work-life balance" is often used to summarize this concept. But I find this term misleading because, for me, work ("Work") is an important and also beautiful aspect of my life ("Life"). "Work-life" balance puts work and life at opposite ends of the spectrum. I would rather call it "Work-Family-Balance" or "Work-Personal-Balance" to emphasize that one serves to generate income to contribute meaningfully to the other.

We all know people who have not achieved this balance: quite a few work 10 to 14 hours a day and sometimes even on weekends. If you're one of them and/or your private and working life is imbalanced, the 90-Day Program will change that for the better.

Create your future with joy

Step 3:
Discover your business idea

"There is no favorable wind for the sailor who doesn't know where to go"
~ Seneca

Once you've identified your motivation and strengths and have carved out enough time, the 90-Day Program gets down to business: working out your business idea to allow you to live the life you want.

Again, you will be given daily tasks to take the right steps in the proper order. It's all about what, how, when, and for whom you want to work.

How much income do you need?

That is a critical question because it determines the minimum your business idea must yield.

Four factors inform your required income:

1. How much money have you already saved?

2. What are your fixed costs for food, rent, education of the children, car, hobbies, etc.?

3. What plans do you have for your future (e.g., children, home, travel)?

4. What does your 401(k) or retirement plan look like?

Obviously, this book is not the appropriate place to discuss the details of retirement provision. There is plenty of literature and advice about this.

In the 90-Day Program, however, you will calculate in concrete terms how much money your business idea has to earn to live the life you want.

How, where, and when do you want to work?

When determining the type of self-employment you seek, consider the degree of flexibility in time and space that you desire:

- **Flexibility:** What are your unchangeable obligations? As a single person, you have far more freedom than if you have to support a family with several children. Maybe you are tied down because you have a family to care for or other commitments that you cannot or do not want to give up. Such obligations make demands on your flexibility (e.g., to be there for a sick child at short notice) or dictate where you can work (e.g., working from home to care for a parent).

- **Working hours:** When would be a good time for you to work, and how many hours would you like to devote to your work? If you want to look after your children when they come home from school, your possible working hours may be limited to four or five hours in the morning and some time in the evening.

- **Travel:** Many people want to escape their jobs to have time for extensive travel. Others want to travel as little as possible and not commute. Whether you dream of working in a completely different part of the world and getting to know the country and its people or prefer to stay in your hometown, it's important to know how mobile you want to be.

The 90-Day Program will guide you to methodically deal with these basic conditions for your dream job before systematically developing it.

How does your calling become a business?

This book is about (re)discovering your very individual calling, appreciating it, and developing it into a business model so that you can test it and — if it bears fruit — implement it step by step. It's only sustainable if you can live from it solely or in conjunction with your partner's income.

There are, therefore, two aspects to your calling and the resulting "profession:"

1. ***What* you want to do for *whom*:** This is what you offer, i.e., the actual content of your activity, and who your customers are. For example, yoga courses for managers, cooking delicious dishes for other people who have little time, or selling knitting patterns for children's clothes on the Internet.

2. ***How* you earn money with it:** This refers to the business model that turns your calling into your earned income, i.e., how your customers pay you. For example, a yoga instruction business can be realized through different business models. You can own and run a **yoga studio** with a punch-card system, or you can offer **online yoga classes** with a monthly subscription and income from online advertising. You can imagine how different these two business models' requirements are, even if you "do" the same thing in both cases, namely yoga instruction.

What types of business models complement your business idea? To give you an overview of the possibilities, I describe the most common business models below and illustrate them with a real example.

Not all business models are equally suitable for all activities, but as a rule, you can use different ones for one activity.

Freelance work ("Freelancer")

Freelance work is one of the most popular business models for becoming self-employed and can be implemented relatively quickly and cheaply. Companies like to use freelancers because they temporarily bring in special knowledge at a lower cost than full-time employees. If you have unique expertise, for example, from your previous job, you can charge quite high fees for it, depending on the industry.

EXAMPLE: Stefan had been employed for years as a developer and consultant at a large software company when his wife wanted to return to her job after maternity leave. They decided to swap roles, which meant he would cut back a bit in his job and care for the children so that she could focus on her career. He had been toying with the idea of working as an independent consultant for a long time to be freer in his project selection and time management. Here is a summary of his experience after nearly four years of self-employment:

"I am glad that I took the step back then, even if it meant a cut in salary, and I have borne the risk of finding customers myself ever since. My wife's new job compensated the lower income. Contrary to my fears, I never actually had problems with enough orders, as I already had a good network of customers. So, the transition was better than expected. I always made sure to have enough long-term maintenance contracts, which gave me a certain amount of planning security. And when a shortage of orders was a threat, I could always get new orders quite quickly via portals like www.gulp.com.

There are, of course, some challenges: If I hadn't been assigned two major clients from my network right at the start, the marketing and sales process would have been difficult as a newcomer because there is a lot of competition from home and abroad. I also had to learn to determine an appropriate fee and to enforce this with the clients. I don't want to hide the fact that it can sometimes be stressful when deadlines are looming, and I haven't made as much progress as planned. That's when I burn the candles at both ends. Of course, my growth as a one-man consultancy is limited, but we have enough income, and my current goal is to have more time than to earn more money."

For a freelance job, you should, therefore, either already have a high level of expertise or special skills that are in demand on the market. Or you should plan enough time to develop a new skill that is not yet sufficiently available on the market—for example, hygiene consultants for businesses during and after Covid.

Retail store

Although building a store is a lot of work, some people love the idea of opening their own brick-and-mortar stores. The location is crucial for success and — especially if it is not ideal — to offer a unique range of products that are worth a physical visit.

EXAMPLE: Reik worked for many years as sales manager of a worldwide wine trade. He realized that he wanted to get out of the corporate world and set up his own business. He knew a lot about wine and opened a wine tavern with a very unique concept: above-average quality wines with a small menu of regional dishes. At the bar counter, orders are placed, wine glasses are filled, and payment is made immediately. The food is then brought to the table a short time later by a server. At exactly 9:45 pm, Reik rings a small bell and visits each table to explain to the guests in a pleasant way that he is about to close, that he also has to go to bed, and he looks forward to seeing them again. As they leave, the guests place their wine glasses on a tray.

The fact that guests were so closely involved in the ordering and serving process had two advantages: Firstly, Reik was in contact with each customer during the ordering and closing process. Secondly, he saved on staff costs and was able to pass on part of the savings to the customers by offering low prices for high-quality wine. The concept was very well received, and although the table set up is quite tight, it's usually booked out to the last seat. The clientele was older sociable people who typically indulge in quality wine and don't drink too much. So, Reik never had to deal with guests who got bogged down at a bar and had to be eased out at closing time. Thanks to the bell, he was able to close the shop usually shortly after 10 pm and was in bed at a reasonable — and healthy — time.

After some time, he and his wife opened a shop offering regional products. They ran their own small coffee roasting business, which was highly appreciated by coffee lovers in the city. When I asked him about the advantages and disadvantages of shops, he said the following:

"At a shop, I can give my guests individual advice, and they can touch the products. This is especially important for customers who appreciate my high-quality regional products, an experience an online shop cannot offer. Especially with products such as wine or regional products, customers enjoy learning about the background of the products. If you then deliver good quality and have an authentic and unique concept, word-of-mouth does the rest. I hardly had to pay for any advertising because I had so many regular customers who always brought someone new with them, who then became regular customers, etc.

As I already knew my way around the wine business, it was particularly important to develop a concept that would save me from working crazy long hours, which unfortunately often happens to pub owners, sometimes combined with high alcohol consumption. I've discovered that customers actually appreciate it when I "kick them out" on time, as it is also good for them not to indulge in wine for too long, despite often asking me if I could make an exception.

In my opinion, the biggest disadvantages of a retail shop are the long working hours, the financial risk, primarily due to the initial investment for renovation, furnishing, etc. and little flexibility. You just have to be there when the customers come. Typically, you also have the challenge of finding good staff and those associated costs. Colleagues of mine have always complained that they constantly have to hire and train new staff. That was hardly an issue for me, as I only had one server and one cook who had been with me for many years. It's worth it to treat them in a decent and appreciative way."

If you have an idea for a retail shop, it's imperative to have a realistic view of the various costs, the often-long-term commitment, and — if you need employees — the personnel issues. If you offer special and unique products (e.g., special dishes, homemade food, or products), your presence will be one of the ingredients for success. People will buy because of you and your enthusiasm, even if the products are significantly more expensive than at a discount store. You are the brand! As soon as you hire someone to sell in your place, you lose that advantage. Your authentic passion for what you offer becomes your brand and why your customers do business with you.

Online store

The sale of products via an online shop is a known quantity to most of us today. It is a business model that can be implemented relatively easily and quickly and usually requires considerably less initial investment than a retail shop. Although there's already a high level of international competition in this space, a profitable business is still possible for the self-employed in a well-chosen niche.

In an online shop, you can sell **goods you have created yourself** or, as a trader, offer the products of others. Due to the strong market position of big online delivery companies such as Amazon, Otto, Zalando, or Alibaba, it is difficult to start a successful online business without fully focusing on a particular customer and/or product group. Your only chance of success is offering something that the big players cannot offer.

EXAMPLE: ZOÉ LU is a fine **example of homemade goods**. ZOÉ LU is a start-up from Munich whose three founders have dedicated themselves to most women's faithful companion: the handbag. The founders identified a problem shared by them and many of their fellow sufferers: not enough space for the many different bags required for different occasions and moving around the entire contents every time the bag is changed.

No other online shop has offered this solution so far: A handbag featuring a diverse selection of changeable flaps and straps. The combination of practical use and creative expression became a wild success and is selling very well.

Strange that nobody has ever come up with this brilliant idea before, isn't it? And the world is still full of such possibilities — to solve an everyday life problem better than before. A good idea is a simple idea. So, if you ask yourself: why has no one thought of this before? You are probably on the right track ...

ZOÉ LU's path from conception to saleable product was not without obstacles. They needed many tests before the product met their requirements. To ensure the product delivered what it promised, the women at ZOÉ LU and their friends wore their favorite bags for weeks. Only then was the first large delivery ordered.

A widespread form of **selling third-party goods is known** as "drop-shipping." Here, the online retailer specializes in certain products that they sell to the appropriate customer segment but leaves all the logistics and warehousing to the manufacturer. That means that the products go directly from the producer to the buyer, and the online retailer himself does not hold or manage the product. That saves on capital and forgoes the stress of complex production, storage, and distribution processes. The online retailer's role is to identify good products, appropriate customer segments, employ effective marketing, and manage payment.

EXAMPLE: When Markus moved to Canada in 2005, he was still employed, but actually always wanted to do something practical with wood. Since the job in Canada did not go as planned, he soon became self-employed and founded the online furniture shop www.ontaria.de[13]

He specialized in Canadian and American furniture of the highest quality, timeless design, and valuable materials, which he sold in Europe. He started with American Art Nouveau furniture by Gustav Stickley, produced in New York for 120 years but could not be bought in Europe — a niche for connoisseurs. That was followed by Canadian garden furniture and Canadian barrel saunas, each made of red cedar, a wood whose properties are superior to other European wood species.

Many of his customers have been to these countries themselves, appreciate the quality, and are willing to pay the appropriate price. Markus opened a shop but found that he was receiving inquiries from all over Europe, and it was not feasible for customers to travel to his shop. So, he closed the shop again and concentrated entirely on the online business.

An online shop's advantages are the potentially high sales volume and repeat customers because you can reach significantly more customers via the Internet than via a brick-and-mortar retail shop.

Thanks to drop-shipping, the effort and investment required are low, and the business model is well established and easy for customers to understand. Marketing channels are also easily and quickly available through online advertising. Still, very high costs can quickly arise here, so that the management of marketing activities is one of the most important and demanding tasks.

You don't want to make the mistake of underestimating the expenses for service, complaints, returns, and potentially high and international (price) competition.

E-books and other digital media

The sale of digital media, such as eBooks, audiobooks, photos, etc. via the Internet has always been a popular business model, open to anyone who can create valuable content. eBooks are one of the easiest ways to get started. You can offer them through existing channels, such as selling them on Amazon for Kindle, or you can choose to distribute them directly through your own website.

A significant advantage is that with a successfully established eBook, you can generate continuous income over a fairly long period without investing a lot of time in it. That is called "passive income."

EXAMPLE: Birgit from Kaiserslautern on the road to independence with eBooks:

"I have been reading books constantly since my childhood, and then I ended up in publishing. The first eight years, I enjoyed my work very much, but when I moved to Kaiserslautern in 2017 and became a parent, my job prospects just didn't work out. I was forced to accept a part-time job through a recruitment agency, but I was unhappy at work and, therefore, also very frustrated in my private life. A friend of mine came up with the idea that I should publish my short stories, which I had been writing for a long time (and which publishers didn't want) as an eBook in a self-publishing format.

In autumn 2018, I published my first title, which, thanks to KDP (Kindle Direct Publishing), can be done in a few minutes. The first title sold better than I expected, so I published four more titles. Today I have more than 20 titles online, earning between $4000 to $6000 a month and am overjoyed to make a living from writing. As a source of income, eBooks have many advantages: they are relatively easy to produce, the cost of distribution is very low, there are many established distribution channels, and good margins are also possible through direct sales via your own website. I sometimes get some real fan mail, but I hardly have to worry about customer service, as platforms like KDP do all this.

As for disadvantages, it should be mentioned that a good book takes some time and the prices for eBooks — and thus the revenues — are sometimes very small.

The biggest challenge is usually to find the right topic, reach the right audience, and write effective advertising texts."

If you have an artistic-creative streak and want to create content such as eBooks, audiobooks, high-quality photos or illustrations, you should consider this option. But you can also use eBooks for other business ideas. They have become a popular way of offering something to customers online and retaining them as customers in the long term. For example, if you work as an independent consultant, you can use eBooks to demonstrate your expertise to your customers.

Online courses

Online courses are a popular business model today, with influential bloggers and online personalities making money.

> **EXAMPLE:** This 90-Day Program belongs to this category of business models. I have chosen this path because it allows me to reach and support as many people as possible.
>
> An alternative would have been that I coach people personally and charge an hourly fee. However, I needed to remain independent of time and place, as I would like to spend more time with my growing children. Thanks to the online coaching offer, I can freely arrange the time I work. For example, I work when my children are in daycare or school or in the evening when they are asleep.

To create an online course, you need knowledge that is rare and valuable, and you have to invest some time in its creation. Usually, you'll need partners for this, such as sound or video recording, website creation, online marketing, etc. You can offer the course online via your own website and/or use existing course platforms such as www.udemy.com. The biggest challenges are to find content that does not yet exist in this form and to differentiate yourself from the competition.

Blogging

Blogging is a popular and widespread business idea whose failure rate — at least on a financial level — is quite high. Most successful bloggers started at some point for fun and interest, and then it gradually turns it into a business model. So, if you don't have any experience with blogging and only want to start doing it to make money, in my experience, the chance of financial success is low.

But if you are truly a thought leader in a subject or very interested and active in a specific niche, you can earn your living via blogging, especially if your cost of living is not (yet) that high. Few bloggers can afford to support a family with children on their own.

It's important that you build up a network of contacts with other bloggers and thought leaders in your field to get support in the relevant communities.

EXAMPLE: Jochen Mai has been running the successful career blog, "Career Bible," for eight years and says:[14]
"For a successful blog you need a coherent business model, a lucrative niche, and usually additional business areas. Very few bloggers live solely from what their blog earns them. That is usually advertising income, but rarely enough. That is why most of them offer other services: They work as consultants, give lectures and seminars that can be marketed via the blog."[15]

He initially ran the blog as a hobby and was still working as a journalist for a **business journal**. It took a few years before his blog began to make a profit.

What is Jochen Mai's advice to prospective bloggers?
"They should have courage, but at the same time, they should assess the entrepreneurial risk. I was able to build my blog over the years alongside well-paid management positions and had the money to invest in my project. But I am also convinced that the network offers numerous opportunities for founders and bloggers. If you have a good idea and really get involved, you have a good chance of success."

Blogging is definitely one of the more difficult business models to consider. You should only consider it if you are a true believer and have a lot of knowledge about and enthusiasm for a niche. You need a lot of time to gain enough readers and become profitable. Monetization through affiliate marketing, for example, is also difficult. Here creativity is required to develop additional sources of revenue.

Real estate

Supposedly, nothing has created more millionaires than real estate. That may be true, but I doubt that millionaires are happier than "normal earners." There are many ways to make money from real estate, including repairing and converting houses, renting out land, or working as a real estate agent or broker.

EXAMPLE: Sabine became a real estate agent more by chance when her children were grown, and she didn't want to return to her old job in product sales. She sold her friend's condominium in her spare time. That worked out so well, and Sabine enjoyed it so much that she continued and looked for more properties to broker.
In Germany, the entry barriers for real estate agents are relatively low, and only six months later, she moved her office from the kitchen table to a small retail shop.

"It was clear to me that I didn't want to be just another real estate agent who just unlocks the flat for prospective buyers and waits for them to sign. That actually works at the moment, because demand is so much higher than supply. But I wanted to advise my clients and have fun working with sellers and buyers. So, I specialized in beautiful properties in good locations, invested a lot of time to make sure that they were shown to their best advantage, and showed them to only a few handpicked prospective buyers, where I had the feeling that they were also genuinely interested.

My sellers appreciate this and recommended me to their friends and acquaintances, usually owners of rather high-quality properties themselves. This way, I have to invest very little money on advertising. A big advantage in marketing real estate is clearly that it can be very lucrative if you have the appropriate knowledge.

Getting into this business is technically very easy. Unfortunately, there are often dubious characters who — often rightly so — confirm the bad reputation of real estate agents. Also, the trade with real estate offers great business opportunities, provided one has the appropriate capital and the necessary credit rating. Here, good relationships with banks, craftsmen, and other service providers are very important to be successful.

On the other hand, there is, unfortunately, a lot of competition, and for years, only a few properties have come onto the market at all. This quickly separates the wheat from the chaff. The challenge is to get a hold of properties because selling is less of a problem in the current market situation in many cities."

Franchise

According to the International Franchise Association (IFA), there are[16] more than 750,000 franchisees in USA, with a current turnover of almost 760 billion USD. In franchising, an existing company lends a business concept to new entrepreneurs for a fee.

Franchisees are independent entrepreneurs who, for a fee, acquire the right to use the brand and know-how of a franchise system.

As a franchisee, you can build up a business idea much faster in an already established market. Many aspects such as marketing, products, sales, and business processes have already been defined, and customer needs have been proven.

However, you are usually considerably restricted in your decision-making scope by the franchisor's specifications. Also, the initial costs are often relatively high, so you should bring some capital with you.

Choosing the right franchisor is a challenge because, in the USA alone, there are thousands of franchise concepts, among which there is something for almost everyone: from cars, gastronomy, fitness, and furniture to tutoring. Nevertheless, it can be challenging to find a suitable franchise to fit your interests.

Test your ideas on customers as early as possible

Step 4:
Develop and test your business idea

The classic business plan has had its day

In the past, new business ideas were planned like a major project in the privacy of a small room. A comprehensive business plan summarized the business idea, the project plan for its implementation, and the expected turnover and profits over five-years. Such a document often comprised 50 to 100 pages and was produced over several months in strict secrecy.

The idea's implementation was then based on the project plan. The company and associated products and services were worked on until the result was presented to the astonished — or unfortunately often uninterested — public with a big drumroll. Only then did it become clear whether there were really enough customers and whether the company was profitable.

Of course, market research was usually conducted beforehand alongside a competitive analysis included in the business plan, with figures supporting a successful launch. Unfortunately, it often turns out that the business offer is not so popular after all, once motivated founders had already invested a lot of time and money in its implementation.

In this case, it's often too late for a second attempt, and the entrepreneurs are forced to lick their wounds, find regular employment again, and replenish their financial means.

Figure 1 shows an example of the steps up to the first customer contact. The left side is an example of opening a yoga studio from one of the most famous German books for professional reorientation[17], on the proper three steps leading up to the first customer test in the 90-Day Program.

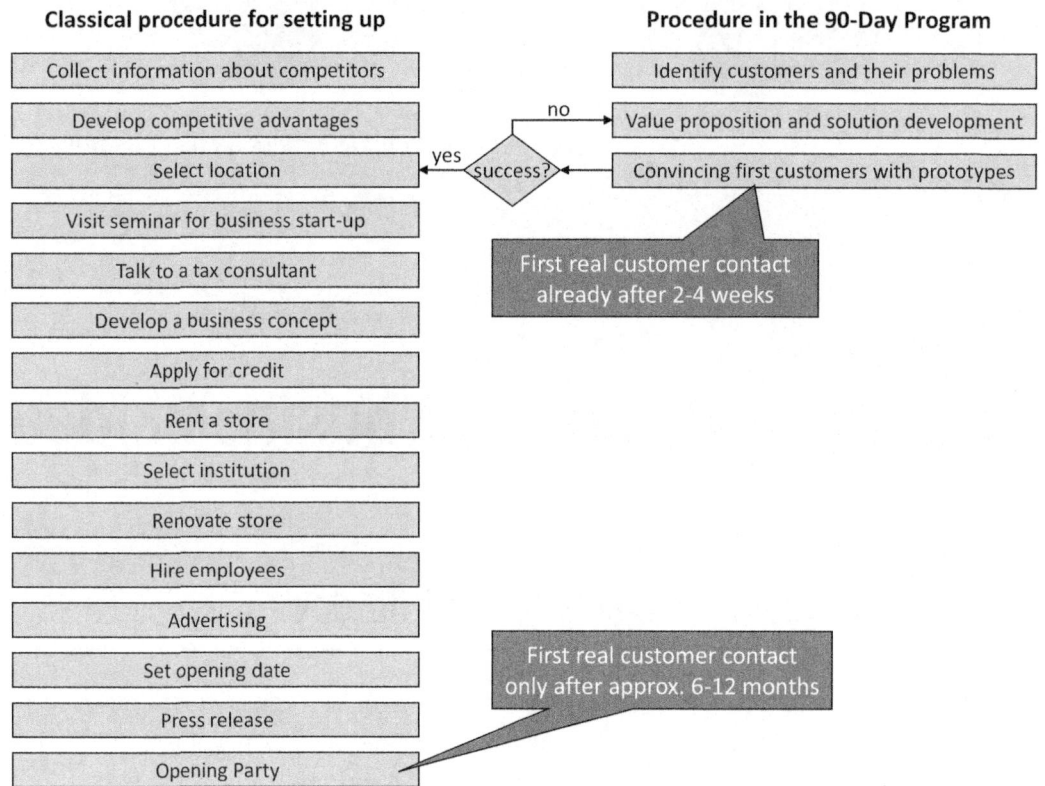

Classical procedure for setting up	Procedure in the 90-Day Program
Collect information about competitors	Identify customers and their problems
Develop competitive advantages	Value proposition and solution development
Select location	Convincing first customers with prototypes
Visit seminar for business start-up	
Talk to a tax consultant	First real customer contact already after 2-4 weeks
Develop a business concept	
Apply for credit	
Rent a store	
Select institution	
Renovate store	
Hire employees	
Advertising	
Set opening date	First real customer contact only after approx. 6-12 months
Press release	
Opening Party	

Figure 1: Comparison of the classical procedure for setting up a company with the procedure in the 90-Day Program

See how everything needed to set up a business is processed one after the other before the customer can enjoy the offer at the very end — or not if the customer's needs are not adequately met. Then the shop is closed after only a few months.

The 90-Day Program turns this process upside down: You will try to sell your idea to customers *as early as possible*. And not in the form of traditional market research, wherein you ask potential customers if they would like product X and if they would be willing to spend Y dollars on it. Far too often, people say "yes" to such questions simply out of kindness. They know that the product doesn't exist yet and that they, therefore, cannot actually buy it.

The customer requires a tangible offer

Instead, during the 90-Day Program, you will make your idea "tangible" as quickly as possible and actually offer it "for sale." You'll tell potential customers that the offer/ product already exists and ask them to make a real purchase decision. After they have already pulled out their wallet or clicked the "buy" button, they will realize that the offer/product is still in the making. You explain the background and offer them a small "compensation" or reward if necessary because they have served as beta testers. This compensation may make them your first customers later. You might offer them first dibs of the product or service and/or at a preferential price. After all, they actually wanted to buy it and are now connected to you through the experience of the offer.

At this point, some people — understandably — have a moral problem because they don't want to lie to others. I feel the same way, that honesty is the best policy and required for my peace of mind. Therefore, displaying tact and a grateful attitude toward your potential customers are necessary here.

The question is: Why would I consciously "lie" to people at this point? Do I want to harm them? Or do I want to offer a benefit to them? My attitude is as follows: I want to develop an offer that people like and hopefully makes the world a little bit better. But how does one *really* know what people *actually* like? Do they *truly* want my offer? I can only find out by confronting them with my offer in a realistic situation. I take what I learn from this "simulation" to provide the customer with what they'd like to have in the future and improve it based on their feedback. So, I don't work *against* the customer; I work *for* them. Of course, I also do this to protect myself from investing heavily in an idea that may not pay off. That, too, is in the public interest.

Our "beta testers" usually understand this explanation very well. However, you must admit as soon as possible that this is (still) a test and that you honestly apologize for having had to mislead the customer for a certain time. If you communicate in a friendly, sincere manner, listen attentively, and take their reaction seriously, it will be a positive experience for you and your counterpart.

If not enough potential buyers are interested, you'll be pleased that you did not invest a lot of time and tens of thousands of dollars in this idea. Instead, you now have enough time and money to improve the idea based on feedback or to come up with a completely new idea.

Because the process is so fast, you can try out different ideas or variations of an idea until you find a convincing offer. And *only then* do you build the necessary business around it because now you know that the customers will actually buy.

This process is called Lean Startup[18] and is so lightweight that you can implement it while you're still employed. You will do this intensively in the second and third parts of the 90-Day Program. The method is fun because creative approaches are required to make the idea tangible for customers.

And it takes courage. You can't procrastinate by hiding behind tasks for months on end, such as looking for financing, looking for property, talking to tax consultants, etc. This process requires courage because it shoots straight to the heart of the matter: convincing real customers of your idea. Sometimes, that can hurt when, for example, you discover that your idea is not (yet) as good as you had hoped.

But remember: "Hope is not a strategy." But that is precisely what the program is designed for: To replace vague hopes with real client feedback to achieve concrete results every day that will help you move forward quickly.

Now that your idea's core has taken shape, the next step is to work out the details and prepare for its implementation. Again, we will proceed as lean as possible, i.e., with little investment of time and money, to achieve a result that you can test on your (potential) customers.

Of customers, offers, and markets: The Extended Canvas

To put your idea into concrete terms, I've developed what I call the "Extended Canvas" for the 90-Day Program, which is a fusion of the *Lean Canvas* by Ash Maurya[19] and the *Business Model Canvas* by Alexander Osterwalder[20].

The "Extended Canvas" is shown in Figure 2. It is a practical, agile tool used to develop and describe your business idea concisely on just one page. It is designed for quick updates and new and ever-evolving insights — for example, after customer tests.

You can now download the Extended Canvas as a PDF at www.how-employees-startup.com/canvas.

Check out Figure 2 to see how it is structured.

Where over 50-page business plans were once written, today's startups work with such a canvas to visualize, discuss, and efficiently develop their idea. The contents are then stuck into the canvases with colorful Post-it's so that they can be easily changed, supplemented, moved, or removed again.

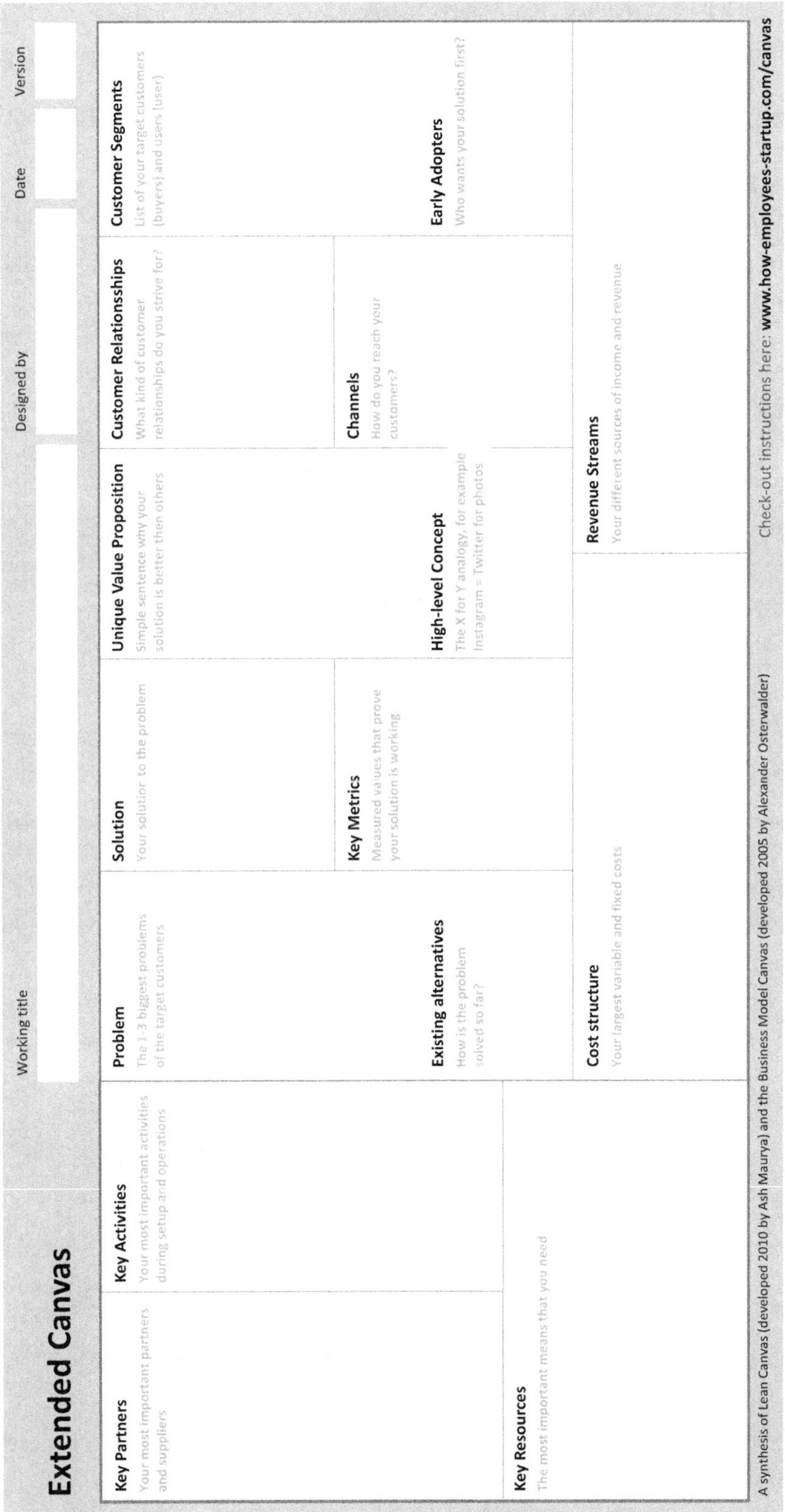

Extended Canvas

Working title

Designed by

Date

Version

Key Partners
Your most important partners and suppliers

Key Activities
Your most important activities during setup and operations

Key Resources
The most important means that you need

Problem
The 1-3 biggest problems of the target customers

Existing alternatives
How is the problem solved so far?

Solution
Your solution to the problem

Key Metrics
Measured values that prove your solution is working

Unique Value Proposition
Simple sentence why your solution is better then others

High-level Concept
The X for Y analogy, for example Instagram = Twitter for photos

Customer Relationsships
What kind of customer relationships do you strive for?

Channels
How do you reach your customers?

Customer Segments
List of your target customers (buyers) and users (user)

Early Adopters
Who wants your solution first?

Cost structure
Your largest variable and fixed costs

Revenue Streams
Your different sources of income and revenue

A synthesis of Lean Canvas (developed 2010 by Ash Maurya) and the Business Model Canvas (developed 2005 by Alexander Osterwalder)   Check-out instructions here: **www.how-employees-startup.com/canvas**

Figure 2: The Extended Canvas for developing your business model

The 90-Day Program takes you step-by-step through the individual fields, starting with your target customers.

1. Customer Segments

You will systematically consider exactly who your future customers are. Are there more women (e.g., yoga studio) or more men (e.g., sports bar)? Which age group is most interested in your offer? What unique characteristics does your target group have (e.g., interested in sports, health-conscious, wealthy, low income, little time)?

At this point, you must define your target group precisely before proceeding forward. Accurately assessing your customer profile makes for successful marketing and selling.

Why not make *everybody* your customer because you'll have a better chance of success? Unfortunately, experience shows that exactly the opposite is true: If everyone is your customer, then no one is your customer. The secret is to focus on a specific customer group (e.g., a yoga studio for stressed office workers, a children's food delivery service for nutrition-conscious mothers, a singing course for musically-challenged people).

2. Problem

After you've defined your customer segment, the next step in the 90-Day Program is to discover your customer segment's problems that a) haven't yet been sufficiently solved and b) are compelling enough that people are willing to pay for its solution. I refer to such problems as "robust problems."

Point a) is important so that you differentiate yourself from the competition, and b) is important since there are many problems to solve, but people are only willing to spend money on a few of them.

In my experience, the biggest challenge for successful self-employment is not to find a brilliant business idea but to find a robust customer problem, i.e., one that is sufficiently large and has not yet been satisfactorily solved. Once you have found such a problem and clearly outlined it, the solution often emerges almost by itself.

3. Unique Value Proposition

Then you can consider the unique way in which you solve the identified problem. This is known as the Unique Value Proposition. It's not yet about what the concrete offer looks like, but what *value* you want to create for the customer.

For example, if you are thinking about a yoga studio *in an industrial park* that helps *stressed office workers (= customer segment)* to *stay healthy and productive despite a heavy workload (= problem to be solved)*, a value proposition could be:

"We help office workers stay healthy, fit, and productive, in only 90 minutes per week."

The value proposition tells the customer the benefit they will get from your offer. It is your "vision" or guiding star, on which all subsequent decisions and activities are based.

4. Solution

The next step is the concrete solution idea that delivers on your value proposition. To continue the yoga example, a solution could be:

"We offer employees <u>a room near the office where</u> they can switch off from their daily work routine for an hour and center themselves to stay healthy and productive."

This solution includes, for example, a yoga studio in a dense industrial area, with weekday classes in the morning, at lunchtime, and after office hours. In addition, small snacks and refreshments could be offered to combine the beautiful (relaxation) with the practical (a healthy snack) for the customers in their daily work.

Another approach to the same value proposition — but this time without a studio of one's own — could be:

"We offer <u>customized yoga courses</u> exclusively for your employees at <u>your office</u>, where they can switch off from their daily work routine for an hour, and center themselves to stay healthy and productive."

Even if the solutions are different and place completely different demands on you and your independence, they both fulfill the same value proposition.

Now you know the four most important aspects you need to clarify at the beginning: Your customer segment, the "robust" problems of these customers, your value proposition to solve these problems, and the solution (your offer) that fulfills your value proposition.

Before you intensively deal with the next fields in the Extended Canvas, you will check and verify the assumptions made so far. If your customer segment doesn't have the problem you've assumed, or your solution doesn't solve the problem or doesn't solve it effectively enough, it's pointless to pursue implementing the idea further. Does that make sense?

In the 90-Day Program, we therefore initially proceed with testing in three steps, which are explained below:

1. Reduce product risk

2. Reduce customer risk

3. Reduce market risk

Reduce product risk

The first step is to check whether your customer segment really has the problem you are suggesting and whether you can really solve it effectively with your solution idea. The risk that these two assumptions could be wrong is referred to as "product risk."

Using the example of the yoga studio: Is a visit to a yoga studio close to the workplace an adequate solution for enough employees to meet their needs for relaxation, exercise, and health?

Since experience shows a high probability that the initial problem/solution does not hit the mark and we, therefore, have to repeat this step several times, it is important that we can find an answer here very quickly with little effort. That is shown in the following diagram on the minimal effort curve (costs & time).

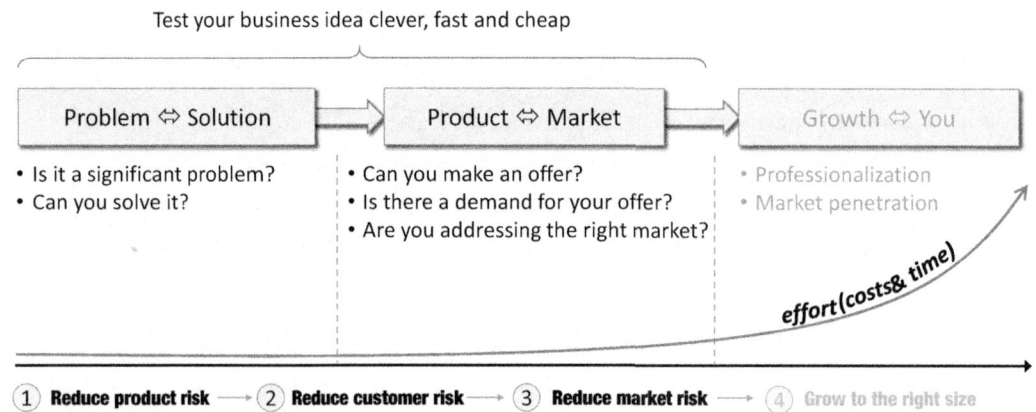

Test your business idea clever, fast and cheap

Problem ⇔ Solution	Product ⇔ Market	Growth ⇔ You
• Is it a significant problem? • Can you solve it?	• Can you make an offer? • Is there a demand for your offer? • Are you addressing the right market?	• Professionalization • Market penetration

effort (costs & time)

① **Reduce product risk** → ② **Reduce customer risk** → ③ **Reduce market risk** → ④ Grow to the right size

Figure 3: The steps in the Lean Startup method with increasing effort (cost & time) over time[22]

Reduce customer risk

The next question is how or where you can approach your customer segment? The chance of being wrong here is what we call "customer risk." So, the following questions are at stake:

- ✓ Where can you approach these people?
- ✓ How can you recognize them?
- ✓ Through which channels can you address them?
- ✓ How can you motivate them to get involved with you and your idea?

We do not only want to check whether your offer is "generally interesting." Instead, we have to find a way to suggest to the potential customer that your offer already exists and to urge them to make a purchase decision, where they pull out their wallet or simply refuses with thanks.

That sounds like a chicken and egg problem: we need a product to inquire about willingness to buy, but we don't want to invest in the product until we are sure that the willingness to buy is there.

As described above, the only thing that helps here is: Fake it till you make it. We have to pretend in a convincing, inexpensive, and non-injurious way that the product exists. Only *after* they have decided to buy, we have to explain to our potential customer that the product is still in the planning stage. In the 90-Day Program, you will learn this step-by-step.

After you have tested the demand in your customer segment as described, there are three options:

1. If you could **confirm** via the test that your customer segment really experiences the assumed problem and your offer with the value proposition has led to real people wanting to pay money for it, you would proceed to further practical implementation of your idea.

2. If you could **only partially confirm** your customer segment and their problems, the next step will be to see if and how you can change the above points to get a more viable business idea. Have you perhaps approached the wrong customers? Or are they the right customers, but you have misjudged their problems? Or are the problems correct too, but you have overestimated their willingness to pay? Then you have to turn the screws and try again until you have found a viable business model, or you reject the idea altogether.

3. If your customer segment and/or their problems **cannot be confirmed** at all, it is time to take a completely different idea and start from scratch. Because this process is so lightweight, you won't have invested much time and money, but you will have learned a lot — good prerequisites for starting a new idea.

Let's assume that it took you a few attempts to find a suitable problem-solution combination for a sufficiently large target group. Have you already reached your goal?

Not quite yet, because so far, you only know that your target group will accept the product, but you don't yet know whether this is a lucrative *market* for you. It could turn out that the production of the product or the provision of the service is too expensive to make enough profit with the price assumed so far. Or the market may exist, but it is not big enough to generate your income in the long run.

Reduce market risk

We refer to the risk that the market is not sufficient as "market risk." To reduce this, you will specify in the 90-Day Program how your offer is to be provided and what profit, i.e., what turnover minus all costs, for example, for rent, employees, materials, electricity, water, heating, insurance, taxes, etc. your idea will bring you.

Maybe these considerations will result in a higher price, and maybe your potential customers will no longer be willing to pay it. In this case, you'd have found a customer problem and a solution, but no market. We only consider a market when the demand is high enough where you can thrive in the long term.

Cost Structure and Revenue Streams

To determine your "cost structure," you will collect all one-off and regular costs in the 90-Day Program, which you will either research (e.g., What will it cost to print 10,000 flyers?) or estimate (e.g., Approximately what will the shop rent cost me?).

You then estimate various sources of income to determine potential revenue and profit. In some cases, there is (initially) only one revenue stream, for example, the sale of wine bottles. However, there are often different services (e.g., sale of wine and events such as wine tastings) or even different ways of paying for them (e.g., a yoga studio membership card for $580/year, a 10-person card for $140, and a one-off trial course for $17). In this case, there would be three different revenue streams to estimate.

How you produce what you offer

After you have defined and validated your offer, your target customers, and your market, you will specify in the 90-Day Program how you want to deliver the offer in concrete terms and what services you need from third parties to do so. To do this, we use the three fields on the left side of the Extended Canvas and the two fields on the right side, as marked in Figure 4.

What comes into view now on the left side are the things you need to create your offer. That includes the key **core activities** to deliver your service, the **core resources** you need to do so, and your **key partners and suppliers ("core partners")** to help you do so.

The right-hand section covers the view to the customers, i.e., what kind of **customer relations** you are aiming for in advertising, sales, service, and customer loyalty (e.g., individual support in a boutique vs. anonymous bulk business at a discount store), and what **channels** you use for what purpose (e.g., a flyer to attract

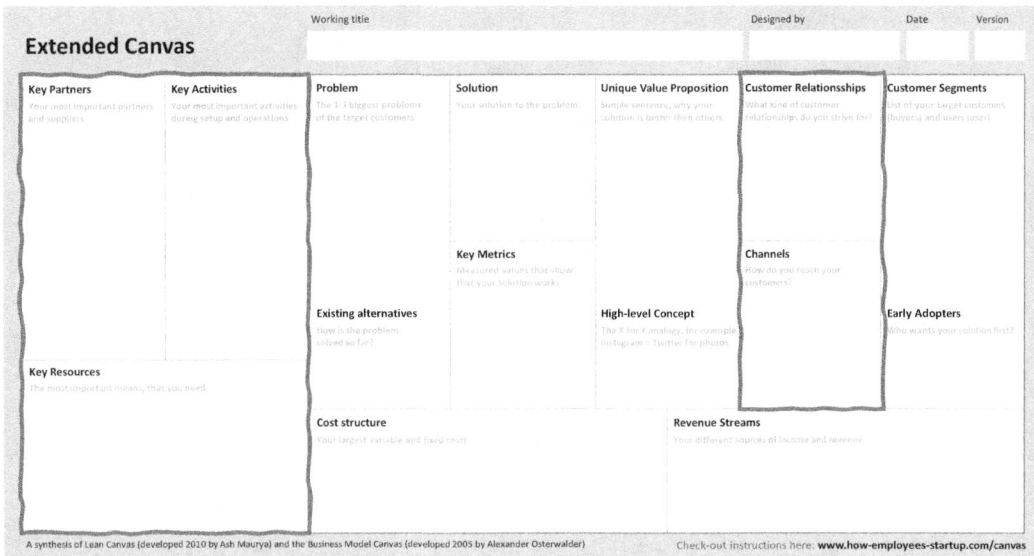

Figure 4: The parts of the Extended Canvas dealing with service provision (left) and customer relations (right).

attention; a website to sell your product/service, parcel service for delivery; service by e-mail and telephone).

In the 90-Day Program, you will work with these fields step-by-step and acquire the information necessary for your business idea. As a result, you'll have defined all the essential aspects of your business model and summarized them clearly on one page.

That offers several advantages:

- ● It gives you a good feeling of **overview and control** when you have put together your business idea with all its facets in such a compact and clear way.

- ● You can **explain** your business model to other people **quickly and easily** and discuss the various aspects with them without losing sight of the big picture.

- ● If you have new insights, you can **adapt** your business model **quickly and flexibly by** replacing, adding, or removing the corresponding Post-it.

Next, we consider which tasks you should entrust to others — and find the right partners for this — so that you can concentrate on what is essential.

To each the task that fulfills him or her — and you.

Step 5:
Do only what you want and outsource the rest

If you know what you want to offer, for whom, and how, it is a question of which tasks you want to limit yourself to. This follows from your calling, which you have (re)discovered in the first two weeks of the 90-Day Program.

We use the "activities" from the Extended Canvas and check which tasks are one-off (e.g., open a bank account, search for property, develop a website) and which are regular (e.g., bill, receive service calls, send out newsletters). For each of these activities, you will decide in the 90-Day Program whether you can/may do them yourself, or whether you would rather outsource them.

I will suggest trusted providers for typical areas (e.g., for marketing, accounting, websites, call centers, company addresses) who will gladly take over unloved and/or difficult tasks for a surprisingly low price.

Did you know, for example, that there are providers on the Internet for the following services:

- Artists who can design a professional **company logo** (from $10) Designers who create all your **marketing materials** (from $100), which you can then print online for little money (e.g., from $20 for 1,000 flyers)

- Contemporary **office workplaces** with complete infrastructure (printers, Internet, drinks, etc.) in beautiful surroundings in co-working spaces (from $5 per day)

- Web developers who create your **website** for you (from $200) **Personal assistants** who take care of everything that can be delegated online, such as Internet research, telephone calls, shopping, presentations (from $10 per hour)

- **Office addresses,** some in well-known top locations, which you can use as addresses (from $20 per month)

- **Secretarial services** that professionally answer the phone on your behalf (from $99 per month)

- And many more things that you probably never dreamed possible!

In the 90-Day Program, you will use service providers who will help you reach your destination quickly, affordably, and successfully. Even though I've been carrying the idea for this book and the 90-Day Program around with me for many years, I've been responsible for the actual implementation (writing the book, working out the 90-Day Program, designing the cover, testing, building the website, advertising, etc.). I have used less than 90 days and spent less than $2900. That was only possible because I focused fully on writing and testing the idea and left the rest to partners all over the world.

Decide consciously where your "Point of Sufficiency" lies

Step 6:
Determine the right scale of your business for you

One task in the 90-Day Program is to calculate how much money you need *at a minimum* to live and how much you need *at most*.

What, why maximum!?

It is unusual in our society to consider an upper limit for your income. Perhaps you are not used to it either, as it is usually about making *as much as possible*. But as explained in the chapter, "Rich is not those who have much, but those who need little," money only makes you happier up to a certain level and, at a certain point, it creates even more dissatisfaction. Even lottery millionaires are only *as satisfied* (or even dissatisfied) after about a year into their winnings as they were before they hit the jackpot.

Remember the story of the fisherman who didn't want to earn more money even if he could? He knew his upper limit for his income, namely enough to *"sleep late, do some fishing, play with his children and take siestas with his wife so that he still has time in the evening to drink wine and play the guitar with his amigos in the village."*

Most of us are not as smart as this fisherman. Once your business idea is successful — and it will be if you do what you really love — there are often further opportunities for growth. Be careful not to become greedy for more and more money and "success" and forget about your satisfaction and happiness. Instead, let others earn the income they need to live and be happy.

What will happen after the 90-Day Program?

What happens to your independence and your life once you've successfully completed the 90-Day Program?

Of course, this depends, first of all, on how far you've come by then.

Over the past 90 days, you've learned a lot about yourself, your calling, your business idea, and your customers. You now know if you can succeed with your idea and if self-employment is really for you.

Usually, there are three possibilities at this point:

1. It may be that **working as a self-employed person is quite different and less attractive than you expected**. Perhaps you've gained a fresh perspective on your previous job or situation and recognize advantages that were not clear to you before and don't want to take such a radical step (right away)?

   If this is the case, then the 90-Day Program has been invaluable because you've learned something new about yourself and gained more clarity. If you are employed, the question now is whether you can improve your job situation to such an extent that you are truly satisfied. Or maybe finding another job is the answer (see Figure 5 below).

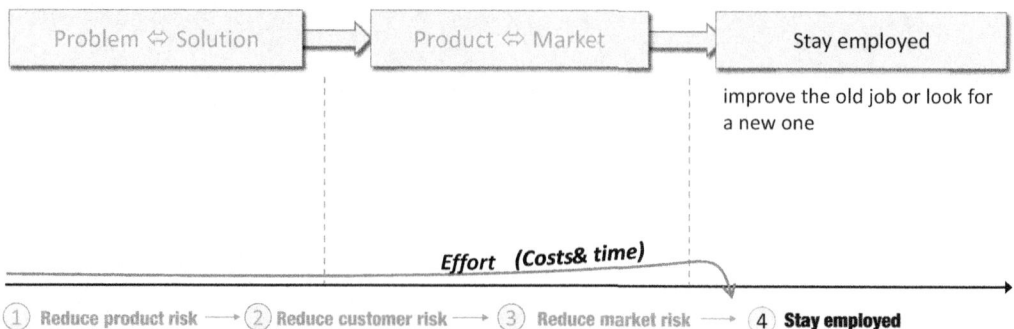

Figure 5: Opting out of the Lean Startup approach when you realize that self-employment is not the right thing for you

2. Perhaps you've found that **you thoroughly enjoy working as a self-employed person, but you haven't developed your current business idea**. Then you'll probably continue to think about how you can become self-employed with a different or modified idea. Now that you're familiar with the process, you'll be able to leverage it even better. To do this, repeat the parts of the program currently on the agenda: Say you've confirmed that indeed, your customer segment experiences the identified problem, you need to create a better solution. Otherwise, you'll need to identify a different problem of your target group or choose another target group (see Figure 6). You now have and know everything you need to do this.

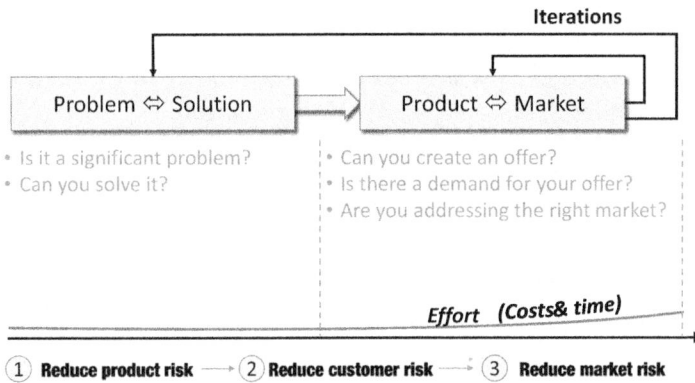

Figure 6: Iterations when the right business model has not yet been found

3. If you enjoy being self-employed and customer tests have shown that **your idea has reasonable prospects of success**, you'll continue on your way and — if you are still employed — perhaps give up your old job in time. Of course, this

Figure 7: The next step to successful self-employment requires significantly more work and effort

depends on how quickly you can earn money with self-employment and how stressful it is for you to continue burn the candle at both ends.

So, after the 90-Day Program, a new phase of your startup begins where your "baby" gradually matures into a real business. Now questions regarding professionalization (e.g., legal form, financing growth, accounting, and tax issues) and further market penetration arise. As a result, you have to step up your efforts (in terms of cost and time), which will become increasingly difficult to manage on a part-time basis.

Excellent information about professionalization is available on websites, seminars, and support services from organizations like the Chamber of Commerce. At the end of the program, you will receive additional sources of information on startup administration.

No matter where you land after completing the 90-Day Program, you can find additional help on the website, www.how-employees-startup.com. As a graduate of the 90-Day Program, many of the offers will continue to be available to you free of charge.

You'll notice that after your initial success, you'll set yourself new goals. Be careful not to let the old patterns sneak back in — keep your original motivation top of mind.

You wanted to spend more time with your children? Then do so, even if it means time spent *not* increasing sales. You wanted more time for your hobbies? Take it and don't give in to the temptation to chase after money or recognition with your new worthy idea.

Everything has a price. And if you want to be rich and famous, the price is much less quiet and relaxed time with your loved ones, just being present in the here and now. And if you enjoy quiet time with your family or hobbies, the price you pay is less income. But I am convinced: it is definitely worth it.

So, now I wish you continued fun and success with your independence. And if you have read this far and still haven't started, what are you waiting for? Start right now!

How?

Go to page 25.

Thank you for your trust and commitment. If you have successfully completed the 90-Day Program, you will also make much, much progress!

If you have any ideas, suggestions, or criticism, I look forward to receiving an email from you at: moritz@how-employees-startup.com.

Best regards

PART II
THE 90 TASKS

Contents

Step 6: Scale your business to the right size for you 227

The second part of this book contains tasks for 90 working days, one for each day.

For each task, you will find the following information:[22]

Reading time		URL to the task on the web

5 Min.   20 Min.   www.hes90.com/1

Processing time		QR Code

Reading time and **processing time** estimates how long you will need to read and then complete the task.

Step 1:
Identify your motivation and strengths

Day 1 — Explore how others perceive you

5 min.	20 min.	www.hes90.com/1	

Today is your 1st day in the 90-Day Program, welcome!

In the first week, we will focus on your strengths and your inner motivation. Today, ask the people around you for their feedback. These are people who know you very well, for a long time, and whom you trust. Typically, these are your partner, parents, grandparents, siblings, old friends, uncles and aunts, neighbors, colleagues, etc.

This is the first task because it takes a few days until you get the answers. We will use the remaining days of the first week for tasks you can do on your own.

Here is your first task:

Write an email to five people from your present and past and ask them for feedback. You can use the following text, change it if necessary, or write your own mail (or letter):

Dear xxx,

I am currently considering my professional future, and I would like to ask you for a favor. You know me very well, and I trust you. Could you help me with feedback on the following questions?

- *What do you think are my greatest strengths and talents?*
- *What have I done exceptionally well in the past?*
- *Which topics do I know particularly well, what would you ask me for advice on?*
- *What kind of job/occupation could you imagine for me, if I could decide completely independent of time, place, and money?*

Can you think of any other points that are important to you and that you'd like to share with me?

It would be great if you could answer by XXX afternoon (date of today, in six days).

I am very much looking forward to your feedback and will be happy to contact you afterwards.

Best regards

...

I can imagine how curious you are about the answers, but please *do not* read them until the day after the deadline mentioned in the mail.

This exercise aims to give you a so-called "external image" of yourself, which you only look at after you have worked out your "self-image" over the next few days. You are welcome to thank the senders directly, but if possible, do not discuss the topic with them until next week.

Have fun writing!

Day 2 — Remembering your childhood dreams

5 min.	40 min.	www.hes90.com/2	

Yesterday you took the first step and immediately asked for support from people who are important to you. Well done!

Today, and over the next three days, you will be occupied with yourself, which means we'll look at your "self-image." We start with the dreams and wishes of your childhood. Do you still remember what you wanted to become as a child?

Here comes the first part of today's task:

Write down the question "What did I want to become as a child?" in your notebook and make a list of the professions you wanted to become as a child.

It's not unusual for children to have very typical children's career aspirations, such as pilot, firefighter, train conductor, football player, dancer, inventor, nurse, millionaire, etc. Children simply do not know many professions yet, but their career aspirations say something about their deeper motivations. For example, "pilots" and "train conductors" would like to travel and/or master technology. The "conductor" also needs to deal with people, while the "pilot" prefers to work in a small team and take responsibility.

Now to the second (optional) part of today's task:

When you are ready, when it's suitable and possible, call your parents, siblings, or grandparents. Ask them which of your career aspirations they remember and laugh together about the past. Then add these career aspirations to your list.

And this is the final part of the task:

Look at the professions you want to do and think about what these professions have in common, write them down in keywords (e.g., work with people, work in nature, and help others be creative).

Here is an example of the childhood dreams of one of my clients:

Career aspiration	Characteristics of the profession
Pilot	Taking responsibility for others, mastering technology, leading a team
Veterinary surgeon	Helping animals, working with animals, understanding how life works
Doctor	Helping others, taking responsibility, working with people, understanding how life works
Astronaut	Discover new things, be a pioneer, master technology, take responsibility
Inventor	Developing new things, developing and mastering technology, being creative

Then mark the two or three characteristics that occur particularly frequently and/or are particularly important to you. Put them in descending order of importance for you.

For our example, it would look like this:

1. Mastering technology (mentioned 3 times)

2. Taking responsibility (mentioned 3 times)

3. Discover new things (mentioned 2 times)

Day 3 — Look at your role models

8 min.	40 min.	www.hes90.com/3

After going back to your childhood, we slowly move forward in your life and next look at your role models.

Who did you admire in your life, and what made these people stand out? Who were your "heroes" in childhood and youth? Which traits did you admire as a young adult, and who do you find fascinating today? What strengths do your role models have?

First part of the task:

Write down the role models in your notebook and write down which qualities you admire in each of them or what distinguishes them from others.

Here is an examples of a client:

- Elon Musk (visionary entrepreneur)
- Neighbor Harald (very nice neighbor, taught me how to do handicrafts as a child)
- Mahatma Gandhi (pacifist leader of the Indian independence movement)
- Keith Harring (artist, street art)
- Richard Branson (entrepreneur)

Please read on only after you have created your own list of your role models.

The second part of the task:

Now examine what your role models have in common and write them down in keywords.

Continuation of the example:

Role model	Properties
Elon Musk	Entrepreneurial, creative, forward-thinking
Neighbor Harald	Creative, friendly, affectionate
Mahatma Gandhi	Peaceful, unifying, represents its interests, takes responsibility, persistent, takes risks, entrepreneurial
Keith Harring	Creative, has kept the child within himself, art for the street instead of museums
Richard Branson	Takes risks, enjoys life, does crazy things, family-oriented, entrepreneurial

The third part of the task:

Then mark the top three features you would like to have from your list (or already have and particularly like about yourself).

Continuation of the example:

- ◉ Creativity

- ◉ Helpfulness

- ◉ Appetite for Risk

Compare the results of this exercise with the characteristics and activities of your childhood career aspirations. Are there similarities? Can you identify the first patterns? Also, talk to your partner, parents, or good friends about your role models, if it suits you. Have fun while you gain exciting insights!

With this exercise, you're dealing with an enlightening topic because your role models represent something that is also dormant in you but may not yet be (fully) developed. What we admire, we often carry within us, but for some reason, we do not live it out like we could.

The opposite is also interesting, by the way: if we detest certain people or actions, it's possible that they act out something that we don't trust in ourselves but would actually like to have. For example, if you find show-offs incredibly annoying, you might want to show a little more of what you can do or toot your own horn. But when you were a child, showing off was so strongly condemned that you learned: "You don't do that!" That's why you may be hiding your light under a bushel too much today. Observe that and think about it; it might be worth it.

Day 4 — Recognize your strengths

5 min. | 20 min. + opt. 30 min. | www.hes90.com/4

Today, we turn to your strengths. These are often qualities and activities that you find particularly easy. The curious thing is that most people are not even aware of their greatest strengths, *precisely because they find them* so easy. When they are praised for it, they often say: "Oh that!? That's nothing special, is it?" Yes, it is! For others, it is, but not for this person, because they find it so easy. The reason it comes so naturally is because it's a great and deeply rooted strength.

So, here's your assignment for today:

What kinds of tasks do you find particularly easy? Write them down in your notebook. Likely, you will not find this easy yourself and not score many points. That is normal and totally okay.

Please create the list now before you continue reading.

Here is a second (optional) part of the task:

If it's convenient for you and others, talk about the question, "What do I find particularly easy?" with at least one person close to you, for example, during a walk, over a meal/coffee, or on the phone. Later, add the most important new findings to your notebook. Often, you'll add one or more points that you don't think are very important. But take them seriously and be happy about them. These are things you do so well that it's just second nature to you! If you don't want to "annoy" the person you trust, just do this exercise on your own.

This exercise completes the picture of your inner self so that over time, it becomes clearer and clearer what you can do, where you want to go, and you will advocate this with increasing force in time.

> **NOTE:** If you are still waiting for replies to your email from day 1, please remind the recipients today. Maybe you just give them a call — this is an excellent opportunity to get back in touch with the people you care about and perhaps speak too little. But don't discuss their answers on the phone; let them send an email to you so that you have it "in black and white." Just call back when you've read the email to say thank you and to exchange thoughts.

Day 5 — Create your "favorite's" list

| 👤 5 min. | 📋 30 min. | 🌐 www.hes90.com/5 |

Today's task is important preparation for the following weeks, especially for the weekends. And it is a task that should be fun!

So, here's the assignment:

Write a list of things that are both good for you and relatively easy for you to do (e.g., taking a nice bath, going for a walk, cooking something tasty, painting a picture, listening to nice music, doing sports, going to the sauna). If you like, you can also divide the list according to things you could do every day (e.g., make a nice cup of tea, read a good book, go for a walk) or more on a weekly basis (e.g., jogging, going to the library) or even monthly (e.g., going to the cinema alone, cooking something especially tasty, eating sushi with friends).

The second part of the task:

Hang this list in a place in your home that is clearly visible to you every day (e.g., on the fridge) and add to it if you can think of anything else.

In the future, pick one, two, or three things from your list every weekend and do them to make sure you're doing well. Enjoy the weekends; switch off the 90-Day Program deliberately because it'll keep you busy enough from Monday to Friday ...

Day 6 — Assemble the external image

⬡ 10 min.	📋 50 min.	🌐 www.hes90.com/6	▦

To date, you should have received feedback by email from the people who are important to you. Today you get to read them!

If you read the answers right away, prepare yourself for the fact that you will feel very beautiful feelings and gratitude. But you may also feel sadness and melancholy because there may be moving words, or you may be reminded of things you have suppressed for far too long. Sometimes you may also be disappointed that a person on whom you have placed great hope only answers briefly and superficially. In contrast, another person might positively surprise you with insights and empathy.

Here now the first part of the task:

Read your answers in peace — several times. When you're ready, consolidate the results so that you see the answers to all four questions summarized. Write down the four questions and the corresponding feedback in your notebook.

Second part of the task:

Now write down all the important points from the feedback to have a list of your strengths and characteristics and then check them: Are there any similarities? Do people from different periods of your life have different impressions of you? What is the difference in feedback between relatives and friends? Now sort the mentioned characteristics by decreasing frequency of mention. How long is the list? The first three to five points are your greatest strengths, and distinctive characteristics as others see them.

Do you agree with all points? Or are there points that surprise you because you did not expect this to be a strength of yours? Trust it: These are things you are good at and known for. If these are qualities that you don't like, you may have lived against your inner convictions for a long time, and it's time that you focus on the things you really want — regardless of what your environment expects of you.

Maybe you are missing some of the qualities you see in yourself? Have others forgotten them, or is this characteristic not (yet) visible to others? Ask someone you trust about this today and listen carefully.

What was this exercise good for? You have supplemented your self-image over the last few days through the perception of others. Now you have a solid base of qualities and strengths on which you can build in the future. Often this means a reorientation because you may be in a professional role that you thought you *had* to do.

Such a reorientation requires courage, and this requires leaving your comfort zone. You probably left your comfort zone the first day you wrote the email or letter.

Tomorrow, we will do another exercise, which is a bit unusual, to slowly get you and your fellow human beings used to the fact that something is beginning to change in you. Does that scare you a little? Sure, because change is always scary. That's how it is, and that's how it will always be. But nothing comes from nothing, and if you continue doing the same things, you will achieve the same results. So, have courage! And be curious and open about what will happen!

Tomorrow, you will take an hour to spend in a café, in a park, or any other public place. Please plan this in advance. If this is not possible for you tomorrow, I've got that covered.

Day 7 — Leave your comfort zone: Making the most of boredom

| 5 min. | 75 min. | www.hes90.com/7 |

Boredom gets a bad rap in our society and should — so they say — be avoided at all costs. Many people seem to be afraid — or ashamed — of not being constantly busy. That is a pity and, in my opinion, even unhealthy because we also need times of idleness and leisure to generate new ideas.

The smartphone, in particular, has become a gap-filler for every occasion. Have an extra minute somewhere? Pull out your smartphone and check ... well, even if there's nothing to check: In the supermarket line, in a café, at a traffic light, or on the train. Everyone is complaining about it, and yet you probably join in too, don't you? But at least for today, that's over!

So, here comes your task now:

Leave your smartphone at home today and take an hour out of your schedule. For this hour, find a park bench or a quiet place outside your house where you can sit comfortably. In bad weather, do this inside, like at a café.

> **NOTE:** If today is really not a good day, then plan a date in your diary for this task no later than within the next five days. Schedule a task in your calendar and activate a reminder to give you enough time to complete it.

Sit there for 60 minutes and do nothing but watch what is happening around you. Avoid starting a conversation, and don't distract yourself; just be there, sit and see what happens. Be aware of your impulses, but don't judge them. For example: "Oh, now I wanted to reach into my pocket again to pull out my mobile phone. Well, it's just not there now." Or, "Geez, people are going to think there's something wrong with me, just sitting here alone and not even doing anything. Maybe they'll think I don't have any friends? Or that I've been stood up? Oh, never mind what people think. I'm fine just the way I am, sitting here now." The principle behind this is called "mindfulness" or "being in the here and now."

Second part of the task:

At the end of the hour, write down your observations and thoughts: What did you notice? Have you discovered insights that are important to you? Was it pleasant or unpleasant, and why? Did this feeling change over time?

On this day (and gladly also on the following days), look out for moments where "boredom" can arise and consciously do not fill them in, but simply sit or stand and perceive what is happening and how you feel. Examples are: sitting in a waiting room without reading one of the newspapers; sitting at a bus stop or on a bus/tram without staring at your mobile phone; waiting at a cash register without distracting yourself; waiting for someone in a café without reading or holding a mobile phone in your hand, etc.

Third part of the task:

At the end of the day, write down your experiences in your notebook and enjoy reflecting on them with someone. In particular, also examine how it felt without a smartphone. That often involves a certain amount of fear ("What if something happens now!?!"), but also the good feeling of having control over yourself again ("I don't need it.").

This exercise raises your awareness of the many influences and the flood of information coming from the outside. You will withdraw from it bit by bit to hear (more) of your "inner voice" again. You need this voice to discover your "calling" and then to develop it consistently.

So, during the 90-Day Program, repeat this exercise every once in a while, when you have short breaks.

Day 8 — Discover your motives

10 min.	40 min.	www.hes90.com/8	

Well, what was the experience yesterday when you were exposed to "boredom?" What did it feel like to be without your mobile phone for a while? Pretty scary how much we're dependent on it, isn't it?

I recommend that you leave your mobile phone at home more often over the next few days when you go out to meet or visit someone, for example. You will have a much more intense time, and you will probably notice, slightly annoyed, how distracted the other person is by their mobile phone. Talk about your "mobile phone experiments". Your counterpart will most likely agree with you and put their mobile phone away immediately.

Now we come to your task for today:[23]

Look at the following 14 pairs of terms, decide spontaneously (without much weighing and thinking) which of the two terms you *like less* and *cross it out*.

Power	Freedom
Curiosity	Recognition
Order	Save
Honor	Justice
Relations	Status
Family	Eros
Success	Enjoyment
Vitality	Beauty
Fun	Silence
Wealth	Harmony
Challenge	Fame
Joy	Idealism
Security	Adventure
Independence	Activity

Please do not continue reading until you have crossed out a term in each line.

Second part of the task:

From the remaining terms, choose the seven that touch you most positively and write these terms in your notebook.

Only read on after you have selected and noted down seven terms.

And the third part of the task:

Now mark the three of the seven terms that appeal to you most and make you feel good. Write these three in your notebook, one below the other, in the order of importance to you, i.e. the most important one is at the top. Do this before you continue reading.

Here is what the three terms mean:

These three terms are your *life motives*, which were described by the motivation researcher Seven Reiss (2009). As a rule, your life motives hardly change. When they do, it's mostly through very drastic experiences.

If you have "vitality" among your top 3 words, please choose a fourth from the other words. Please do not continue reading until you have done so.

And the last part of the task for today, if you had "vitality" in the top 3:

The desire for vitality is a sign that you are quite exhausted. Take extra good care of yourself now; you are the most important thing in the world! You can only be there for others if you have taken good care of yourself. So, take special care of yourself, your body, and your soul!

This exercise enriches your understanding of yourself with rational aspects that your left brain understands well. It complements the first few days' exercises, which were aimed more at your creative right brain.

Day 9 — Make a wish

10 min.	50 min.	www.hes90.com/9	

You will enjoy today's exercise! Today, for once, life is a bowl of cherries and lot's of beer and skittles, because, on this day, you can wish for anything!

Imagine a fairy godmother grants you three wishes. Anything is possible, however irrational it may be (except more wishes, of course). This may have to do with your professional life or with entirely different things.

Your first task for today:

Think about your chosen three wishes and write them in your notebook. Please formulate the wishes as short text, not just as a keyword. Be spontaneous and don't think about it too much; just write them down.

Second part of the task:

When you are finished, take a closer look at the wishes and think about what they stand for. For example:

- More time? What would you like more time for? What would you do with your free time?

- Or more financial freedom? How would you use this?

- A fulfilling profession? What would make a profession fulfilling for you? What would the working day look like? Where and how long do you work?

What are the needs behind your wishes? For each of the three wishes, write down what comes to your mind, what they mean to you, and which areas of your life are addressed by them (family, job, partnership, time for yourself, hobbies, community, etc.)

If you've understood and completed your three wishes quite well, then take a short break, get yourself a tea, a coffee, or a small snack, for example. You can also just get up for a short time, stretch and stretch with pleasure before continuing.

Third part of the task:

Now you are allowed to wish for five different lives, in addition to the one you are already leading today. Imagine that you could be whatever you want: a movie star, a monk, a gardener, a space traveler, a billionaire, the world's best teacher, a heart surgeon, etc. What would that be?

We are not here to deny or denigrate your real life. It's about letting your imagination run wild: Which five lives would you choose? Write these five in your notebook.

This exercise is designed to help you look beyond your current thinking and think "out of the box." That is important for finding creative ideas for your future occupation. To be creative, you must think far beyond the norm, preferably to the extremes. In the end, the result will be somewhere in the middle between the status quo and the extremes.

Fourth part of the task:

Now choose the life you find most attractive, regardless of all the secondary conditions (income, family, place of residence, your body, etc.), no matter how crazy it sounds! Mark this life with a "1." Which one would be the next best? Write a "2" there, etc. until you've put them all in the order of your personal preference.

Please read on only after the list has been numbered.

The last part of the task:

The life you put first contains what you are missing most today. Even if that sounds impossible or even threatening at first — don't worry! You should not throw away your old life right now.

It is more a matter of (re)integrating the aspect you are currently missing in your life more intensely and, in return, gradually letting go of things that you are still doing but which don't really satisfy you.

So, if you're a banker or baker at the moment but would actually prefer to be a rock star, then first find something where you can stand on stage, maybe in a band or a theatre group. If you are a father of three and would like to explore the history of the world as an archaeologist, plan your next holiday with your family so that you can go on a search for clues. If you start to follow your motivation, new and unexpected possibilities will gradually emerge.

Day 10 — Write your own funeral eulogy

| 7 min. | 50 min. | www.hes90.com/10 |

Today's task may sound somewhat morbid, but it is very insightful. Life gains value and significance in the face of death. Unfortunately, death has been somewhat ignored in our society and plays a role in an utterly alienated form, mainly in the media as entertainment.

> *"Reminding myself that I will soon be dead is the most important tool to help me make the big decisions in life. ... Remembering that you are going to die is the best way to avoid the fallacy that you have something to lose. You are already naked. There is no reason not to follow your heart."*
> ~ Steve Jobs,[24]

Your task for today:

Take time for yourself today and write the speech you would like to hear about yourself at your funeral. What would your life have been like if it had been terrific?

If you feel that you cannot or do not want to do this, I have an alternative for you below.

Imagine your funeral in detail: a beautiful ceremony to your liking, all the people who were important to you in your life have come to say goodbye to you. You are laid out with many flowers around you, and everyone thinks of you wistfully and with love.

Then someone stands up, goes forward, and gives a beautiful and authentic speech about you and your life as you would wish it. This speech contains all the good you have done so far, also names in loving words the weaknesses and the mistakes that belong to your life so far and describes in the most beautiful colors how you've lived the rest of your life from today on. What should people remember about you?

Write the speech and include the positive qualities, strengths, achievements, knowledge, etc. that you would like to hear about yourself. Let your imagination run free, and don't limit yourself — neither spatially, financially, nor what seems possible today. It should be exactly the kind of life you want for yourself, which is described in the speech. Have fun!

Alternative task:

Imagine your 80th birthday: You are healthy and fit. Your friends and family have organized a fabulous party precisely to your taste. All the people who have been important to you in your life have come to celebrate you. You sit at the table of honor with lots of friendly faces around you. Then someone stands up and gives a beautiful and authentic speech about you and your life as you would like it to be. This speech contains all the good things you have done so far and names in loving words the weaknesses and mistakes of your life. It describes in the most beautiful colors how you've lived and worked for the rest of your life from today until your 80th birthday.

Perhaps the person will briefly describe the changes you have gone through and then tell you what you've consciously chosen to do and how you have achieved all the good for yourself and others. What do you wish the orator to report in the future?

What is this exercise good for? In the speech, you will find things that are really important to you. This works especially well in the eulogy because there is no point in worrying about what others expect you to do when you are dead. But even on your 80th birthday, you are already in a phase of life where you no longer have to do many things that might still be a burden to you today. That is liberating.

In this way, a mission statement is created from which you can intuitively deduce how you should behave, what is important to you, and what is less important to you than it seems today.

Day 11 — Unite your motivation, strengths, and dreams

15 min.   45 min.   www.hes90.com/11

Have a second look at the results of the last two weeks at your leisure and with a little distance: The image of the people you trust; your self-image in terms of motivation and strengths; your childhood dreams and what you learned from them; your favorite activities that are good for you, your motives, your dream life, and your own eulogy.

Your task for today:

Below you will find various forms of intelligence described in the literature. Have a look at them in detail and think about which one suits you best:[25]

- ☐ Verbal-linguistic intelligence (spoken and written)
- ☐ Logical-mathematical intelligence (abstract logic and numerical thinking)
- ☐ Spatial-visual intelligence (ability to think in images and visualize accurately)
- ☐ Physical-aesthetic intelligence (ability to control the body and handle objects)
- ☐ Musical intelligence (ability to make music)
- ☐ Interpersonal intelligence (ability to understand and relate to others)
- ☐ Intrapersonal awareness (self-confidence)
- ☐ Naturalistic intelligence (understanding nature)
- ☐ Existential intelligence (understanding the deep questions of life)

What forms of intelligence do you have when you think about the findings of the last ten days? Mark one to three forms of intelligence that best describe you.

Second part of the task:

Look at the following list of skills and mark the three to five skills that best suit you.

- ☐ Communication skills
- ☐ Empathy
- ☐ Social intelligence
- ☐ Emotional intelligence
- ☐ Leadership qualities
- ☐ Persuasiveness
- ☐ Ability to analyze
- ☐ Critical thinking
- ☐ Strategic thinking

- ☐ Problem-solving skills
- ☐ Planning skills
- ☐ Organizational skills
- ☐ Technical skills
- ☐ Manual skills
- ☐ Honesty
- ☐ Integrity
- ☐ Creativity
- ☐ Reliability

- ☐ Responsibility
- ☐ Artistic skills
- ☐ Written skills
- ☐ Public speaking skills
- ☐ Pedagogical skills
- ☐ Project management skills
- ☐ Physical coordination
- ☐ Humor

These exercises are a further supplement to your right, rational brain so that you develop a balanced view that involves your whole body and your full potential.

If it suits you, discuss the result with someone close to you, and consider where else your particular forms of intelligence can be seen.

Third part of the task:

Now you consolidate the results of the last ten days. To do this, take a blank page in your notebook or — if it is rather small — a blank letter-sized page.

Write your name in the middle of the page and write the results of the last eleven days branching off your name to create a mind map. In figure 9 you can see an example from Marcel, one of my coachees.

Mastering technology
Taking responsibility
Discover new things

Features of my
childhood dreams

Motifs

Freedom
Curiosity
Challenge

Creativity
helpfulness
Risk appetite

Features of
my role models

My three
wishes

Buy a house in Bonn
Happy marriage
Successful self-employed

Marcel

My desired life

As a free inventor
I develop successfully
Ideas for a clean
Environment

Developing ideas
inspire me
Initiate projects

Whats easy
for me

Forms of intelligence

Logical-mathematical I.
Spatial-visual I.
Interpersonal I.

Listen well
Positive thinking
Packing things
Craftsmen & Handicrafts

External image

Skills

Ability to analyze
Creativity
Manual skills

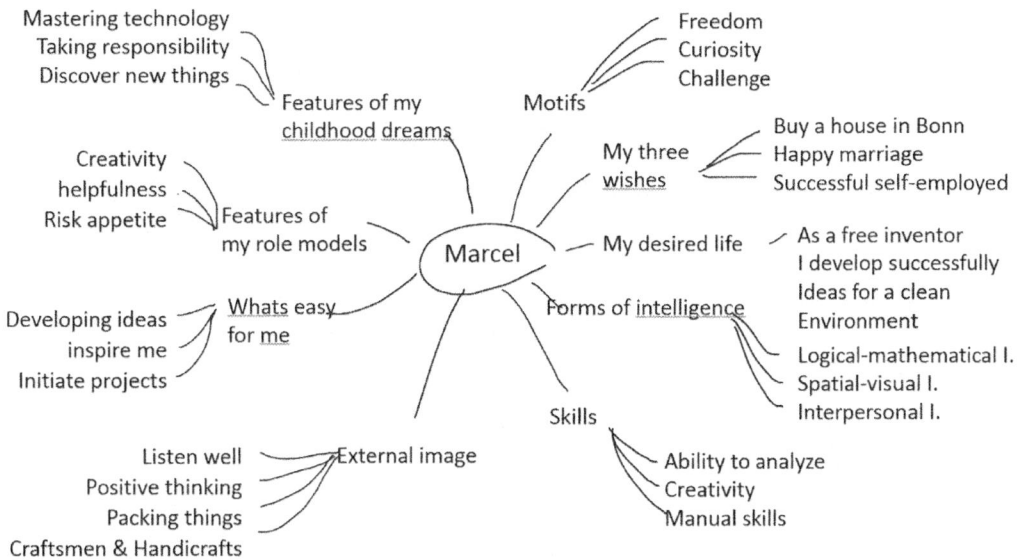

Figure 8: Example of MindMap by Marcel

Last part of the task:

Then consider alone or together with your confidante, which activities with your combination of motivation, strengths, motives, wishes, intelligence, and skills are particularly suitable. For example, if you have musical and interpersonal intelligence, you might be a good music teacher. If you have spatial and naturalistic intelligence, you might be a good gardener, landscaper, etc.

Write down all ideas, no matter how crazy they are, in your notebook.

Figure 9 uses Marcel as an example to show how well his desire to become a "freelance inventor" fits in with his strengths, motives, and the way he sees others.

Mastering technology
Taking responsibility
Discover new things

Features of my
childhood dreams

Creativity
helpfulness
Risk appetite

Features of
my role models

Developing ideas
inspire me
Initiate projects

Whats easy
for me

Marcel

Motifs

Freedom
Curiosity
Challenge

My three
wishes

Buy a house in Bonn
Happy marriage
Successful self-employed

My desired life

As a free inventor
I develop successfully
Ideas for a clean
Environment

Forms of intelligence

Logical-mathematical I.
Spatial-visual I.
Interpersonal I.

Skills

External image

Listen well
Positive thinking
Packing things
Craftsmen &

Ability to analyze
Creativity
Manual skills

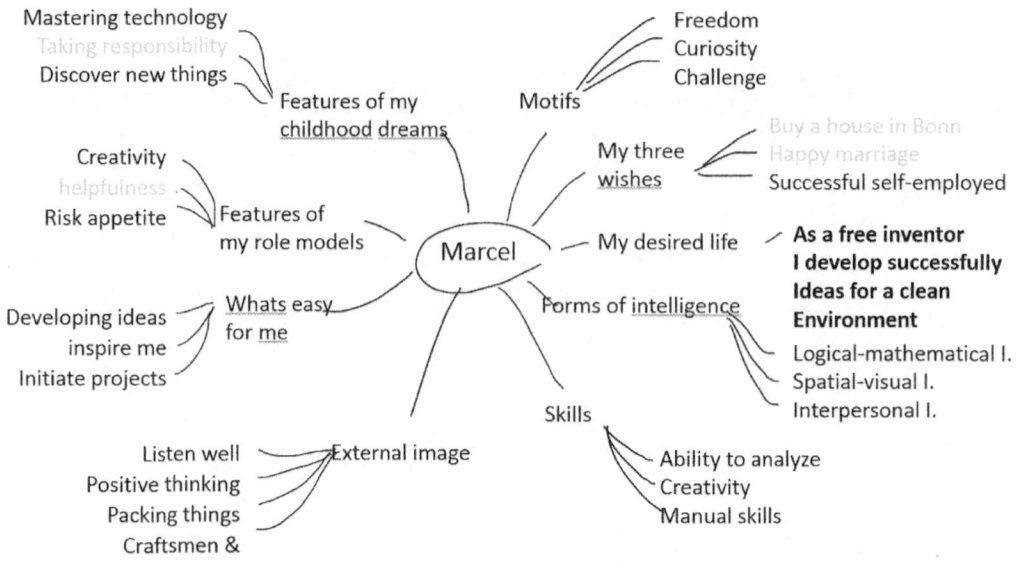

Figure 9: Example of MindMap by Marcel about his dream job

Marcel then actually set up his own business, initially on his own, and later a colleague from his old employer in the process industry joined him as a partner. He now lives from engineering and consulting projects, which he carries out independently for industrial customers. Thanks to his experience and contacts from his career with a medium-sized company in North Rhine-Westphalia, the transition to self-employment was easier for him than he had feared.

When you're done, close your notebook, do something completely different and sleep on it for a night. Pay attention to what you dream about tonight — something interesting might come up, but it doesn't have to.

Step 2:
Create time for your business idea

Day 12 — Tame your smartphone

10 min.   30 min.   www.hes90.com/12

Previous assignments have usually not taken up much more than 60 minutes per day, even though you have probably thought a lot and repeatedly about the topic and/or talked to someone about it. During the 90-Day Program, you will need more time, later on, so you'll start to free up or take this time now.

Anyone who says, "I don't have time," is actually expressing, "I don't care enough." So, you will have to "take your time" to reach your goal.

Your first task for today:

Identify your time-eaters and make them harmless. To do this, go through your typical everyday life in your mind and list in your notebook all the things that eat up your time, energy, or attention:

- What things cost me time (whether useful or not)?

- What things draw my attention (e.g., seeing/listening to the news, TV running — possibly in the background, notifications that "pop up," etc.)

- What costs me a lot of energy (e.g., conversations with certain people, unfinished business that gnaws at me, commitments that I don't even want, etc.)?

- What hidden benefits, if any, do I get from these things (e.g., when I see social media news or likes, does it make me feel "good" and "in demand")?

- What could I do to eliminate all or at least part of the time-eaters?

Please read on only after you have listed all your time-eaters and answered the five questions.

This week we will first concentrate on the time-eaters, which were sold to us as useful helpers for work *and* diversion: smartphones, social media, computers, television, video games, etc.

Today, you're going to start with the first important step: your smartphone. Let's face it: in modern life, it's the scourge of our time!

Second part of the task:

Take 20 minutes today and implement the following steps:

- ✓ Uninstall the app you use most often to distract yourself (often this is Facebook, Instagram, YouTube, etc.) Don't worry; you can install it again in a few days/ weeks if you really feel like it.

- ✓ Deactivate the "notifications" for all apps and activate the notifications again in the next few days selectively only for those apps that are of practical use to you in everyday life.

  - ▸ For Android: "Applications" or "Apps" settings. Select the app you want to disable notifications from and follow the instructions.

  - ▸ For Apple: "Messages" or "Notifications" settings. There, switch off the settings for the desired apps.

Third part of the task:

In addition, do the following exercises every day as a weekly task:

- ✓ Consciously leave your smartphone at home when you meet people and enjoy the new freedom. You arrange a time and place beforehand, and then it's off. If you really need your smartphone, for example, for your public transport ticket, set it to flight mode throughout.

- ✓ In case you actually take your smartphone with you when you leave the house:

  - ▸ Don't take pictures with your smartphone but enjoy the moment as it is.

  - ▸ Don't show your friends photos/videos on your phone, but rather *tell* them about what you want to show them.

  - ▸ Attention! You must leave your comfort zone here: If someone wants to show you something on your smartphone, tell him or her that you're incorporating less screen time into your life and that they should instead tell you about the experience. Many people will be amazed and impressed and ask themselves why they haven't done that before ...

With this exercise (and the following days), you will achieve three critical goals:

1. You create the time you need to develop and implement your ideas without losing the efficiency in your current job. On the contrary: Your productivity should increase during the 90-Day Program!

2. You withdraw yourself from many influences and information that distract you from yourself and are not good for you.

3. You regain control of your life, which will give you the strength and stamina to realize your idea.

Day 13 — Tame the emails

5 min.	30 min.	www.hes90.com/13

Today's task is only relevant for you if you are bombarded by too many emails. If this is not the case, you have the day off.

The biggest time guzzler during work is usually email. What a wonderful invention, but also what a curse!

The problem is that most people check their emails several times a day and again and again, only to respond immediately. That keeps people busy and gives them the (often deceptive) feeling that they are accomplishing something. Because almost everyone thinks and works this way, more and more emails are created, with ever-larger distribution lists, to which people then react again to feel busy.

Here is your task:

As of today, you are getting out of this problematic club! For the next two weeks, please adhere to the following iron rule:

Emails are only and exclusively checked at 11:00 am and 4:00 pm and answered within 30 minutes.

This way, you start your working day directly with your actual work and don't spend half the morning, "just checking your emails."

Explain to your colleagues why you are doing this by activating the following automatic email reply for one week:

Ladies and gentlemen,

Due to the high workload, I read and answer my emails daily only at 11:00 and 4:00.

If you urgently need help that cannot wait until 11:00 am or 4:00 pm, please call me at Tel. xxx-xxx-xxx.

Thank you for helping me be more efficient so that I can better support you.

Best regards,
[Your Name]

During your dedicated email time (e.g., from 11:00 am to 11:45 am and 4:00 pm to 4:45 pm), you first mark all emails that, at first glance, are obviously irrelevant to you as "read" or delete them immediately, then they are moved to the trash.

Now go through the emails and sort them according to specific criteria before you reply:

- Are you only on cc?
  → Skim the title and, if applicable, the content to assess whether it is relevant for you. If no, mark it as "read;" if yes, read it and only derive tasks for you if they are essential.

- Are you just being informed?
  → No answer

- Are you being asked something?
  → You are the right contact person. Think briefly about whether the question can be clarified more quickly and better with a short telephone call and make a note of it. If you are the right contact person and can answer the question in less than two minutes by email, then do so. Otherwise, plan the answer (preferably by phone to answer counter-questions immediately, discover other things "between the lines," and maintain the relationship).
  → You are the wrong contact person. Forward the email to the right person, with the original "contact" in cc: and just write:
  "Hello [name], can you please do this for [contact]? Thanks!" Greetings, [your name].

With this procedure, you will save about 80% of the time spent on email.

Practice this discipline daily. What is becoming increasingly important now: You need to know what to do with your freed-up time. Many people don't know what to do with their free time and start to fill it up with "being busy" again. But you know how you want to use your time: developing your own ideas, to push them further, and to take care of yourself and your life.

This exercise will get you out of the email grind in which so many people are stuck because it gives the deceptive feeling of being busy and creating something. To successfully implement your own business idea, you need to focus on real benefits for yourself and your customers and no longer just on "being busy."

Day 14 — Renunciation of TV watching

| 5 min. | 30 min. | www.hes90.com/14 |

Do you binge-watch or frequently sit in front of YouTube or other video websites? Then you have a lot more time than you admit! For the sake of simplicity, we'll summarize all these time-eaters below under "TV."

Your task for today:

Start by restricting your television consumption. If you watch every day, decide now that you will only allow yourself one or two hours of "sprinkling" once or twice a week at most. On the other days, use the time for yourself and your business idea. You will be surprised how quickly you make progress!

Today and for the next two days, television will be canceled. Use this time to decide with the people you live with on how, when, and for how long you'll be watching television.

If you live alone, consider completely canceling streaming services like Netflix, Hulu, HBO, etc. That way, you not only have more time but also a little more money.

Consider this: You make time for things that are important to you. Do you want to prioritize television over actively shaping your life and finding a job that makes you happy and satisfied in the long run?

By the way, the same applies to listening to the radio and podcasts. If you like the radio as background music, you can leave it at that. But if these shows are inundated with news, commercials, etc., then try living without them for a week starting today. At the very least, these things draw your attention away from other — more important — issues. This content (frequent negative and disturbing news items) also can impose a negative mindset and costs you precious energy. Important news isn't going anywhere and you're not going to miss it because media repeat "breaking news" ad nauseum. So, you can relax knowing that if you missed a news item, it was probably not so important for your life after all.

This exercise will make more time available for your most important project and reduce information overload. Notice how this gets you in touch with your inner voice and intuition over the next few days.

Day 15 — Leave your comfort zone and be upright

10 min.   20 min.   www.hes90.com/15

You are undoubtedly aware of how much a person's outer posture says about his inner posture: he is *upright* and *steady*. It shows *backbone*. He looks *buckled*. She lets her *head hang down*. He has *stooped to* his fate.

These expressions and phrases say something about the inner state of the person. Disappointments and struggles that are not processed are expressed in body language, for example, slumped shoulders or slightly bent over.

In fact, it works both ways: If we change our *physical* posture, it also affects our *mental* posture. If you want to implement your business idea, you need sufficient stamina, assertiveness, self-confidence, and a clear vision. From now on, you'll practice this daily over the coming weeks.

Here is your task for today:

Stand in front of a mirror and consciously change your posture: First of all, round out your back a bit, let your shoulders and head hang, and bend your knees slightly. Stay in this position for a few moments and observe how you look and feel in the mirror. A sad sight, isn't it? Even if I didn't tell you to control the facial expressions on your face, you probably look a little sad and upset now.

Now change your position and stand up straight. Imagine that your sternum is pulled up slightly, which will automatically curve the hollow of your back a bit (which is not bad, as is often falsely claimed), and your shoulders are pulled back. Now your head or chin will probably feel a bit high, which makes you feel "stuck-up" and "looking down from above." Pull your chin down a bit, as if you want to make a double chin (don't worry, it won't show!). This stretches your neck, which is good for the neck. You can also imagine that a thin, strong thread is tied to the highest point of your head and pulls you towards the sky.

Now walk around the room in this position. Feels weird, doesn't it? On the one hand, quite good, because you strut upright like a nobleman at court. On the other hand, also a bit unusual and stiff — and in your eyes may be a bit arrogant or *overbearing*?

You will need self-confidence, pride, sincerity, and assertiveness for your successful independence! And this is the point where you now fully move out of your comfort zone: Am I really allowed to be so self-confident? Doesn't that make me arrogant? Won't others immediately see how I'm faking it? Yes and no!

Yes, others will perceive that you appear more upright, confident, and "committed." No, they will not perceive you as "artificial." On the contrary, many will note their own bad posture, and many will also become more upright, consciously, or unconsciously.

The same applies to sitting. Grab a chair and sit on it like you usually do. Your pelvis has probably fallen back a little, and your back has rounded. Exaggerate this position a bit by making your back a bit rounder. Your shoulders will probably also round out now, and your head will hang forward.

Now slide your buttocks on the chair up to the front edge, so you only sit on the first third of the seat. Tilt your hips forward until you sit on the two so-called "sit bumps," and your back is straight or curved slightly in the hollow of your back. Put your hands under your buttocks for a moment so that you can feel the ischial tuberosities. This upright and active sitting position may also feel different but looks a little less "arrogant" than the upright (and healthy) position you were in before.

Your task from now on is to practice this posture as often as possible in standing and sitting: When you "strut in" at the bakery, when you sit with your family at the dinner table, when you enter your workplace, when you go shopping when you cook, etc. Be prepared to be asked about it. When you eat, some others at the table may imitate it — sometimes unconsciously — because it stands out so much when someone sits so upright. Do not let this make you feel insecure. Feeling and accepting this is precisely the challenge because, remember, this was outside your comfort zone until now!

Why this exercise? If you want to become independent, your attitude toward yourself and others is of central importance. You will radiate success and *stand by* yourself and your idea with full conviction. That is what you'll practice with this exercise — not only today but in the future every day, if possible! It's also very beneficial for your health — and your charisma.

Day 16 — Restrict the telephone

15 min.	15 min.	www.hes90.com/16

Today's task is only relevant if you make a lot of phone calls in your job. If this is not the case, then you have today off.

For four days now, you've been freeing yourself from the clutches of your smartphone. I hope you can already feel the difference and enjoy your increasing independence. You probably also notice how often you think about your smartphone, how much you want to look at it, and how hard it is to remember to *not* take it with you when you don't need it.

Do *not* give in to these impulses. You can't do that? How will you manage to become successfully independent if you can't even control this aspect of your life? It may sound trivial, but this is an exercise in discipline and focus — you need both on your journey to more freedom, independence, and self-determination.

So, for today and over the next few days, the good old landline phone, which many people have at home or in the office, will be added.

We humans can hardly bear it when our phone rings, and we don't answer it. Who might that be? Could it be something important? Oh, someone wants to talk to me, how nice! Is it perhaps good news? Or is it bad news?

Surely, you get annoyed at the doctor's office, waiting for the receptionist to get off the phone to help you. It's a bit like someone cutting in front of you in line, isn't it?

Don't let a phone cut in front of the things that are really important to you. If the caller has a critical request, they will definitely get back to you. And if not, that's fine.

That is your task for today and the next weeks:

From today, if you are engaging in focused work, switch your phones to silent or forward them to your answering machine. Then listen to the answering machine and respond to the calls ASAP to let people realize that they can rely on you.

If you forget to switch your phone to silent or redirect it, just let it ring. You'll probably have to leave your comfort zone to do this, but it's an excellent exercise to focus on yourself and not be there for everyone at all times.

If a somewhat annoyed colleague stands at your door a few minutes later and asks you why you're not answering the phone, say calmly: "I was and am currently absorbed in work and would like to finish it without interruption. I would've called you back afterward (or would have come by). What time would suit you best?"

Get into the habit of greeting callers and visitors properly when you want to get things done. If you are busy and start with a "Hi, how are you?" don't be surprised if a conversation develops while you're sitting on hot coals because you didn't really want to talk at all; you just wanted to "be nice." But this is not nice, because you are conveying the wrong message, namely: "Hi, I have time for you." Save that for those moments when you've just finished something important and feel like making small talk.

The motto is here: If you are not interested in the answer, don't ask the question! This is another healthy chance to move out of your comfort zone, learn new habits, and be more engaging!

Much more honest and productive is: "Hi, what can I do for you?" If the caller/visitor can briefly and concisely express his or her wish, you write it down and say goodbye with the promise to take care of it later. If the person you are talking to insists on engaging further, in a friendly manner, say: "[Name], I'd like to give 100% to you and your issue, but right now I'm in the middle of a job that I'd like to finish. Is it okay if I contact you afterward?"

Second part of the task:

At the end of this series of exercises, write down the most important resolutions for more efficient work with your smartphone, email, etc. as keywords on a piece of paper and place it at your workplace. Don't hang it on the wall or as a Post-it somewhere because it will become invisible to you. Leave it at your workplace, even if it might get in the way.

Day 17 — Organize yourself

| 15 min. | 30 min. | www.hes90.com/17 |

In the last few days, you have tamed your technical time-eaters. Today you are starting to improve your work organization to free up time and become more effective.

Here is your task for today:

First, take a look at the time-eaters in the following table. Which ones apply to you and your everyday life, and to what extent? All habits, even the bad ones, benefit you, even if it sounds absurd and isn't easy to recognize at first glance. Do you understand the benefit behind your time-eaters? The table gives you a suggestion for each one.

Time Eaters	Benefits
Lack of concentration/ do too much at once	Feel irreplaceable?
Perfectionism	Get recognition? From whom?
Putting off unpleasant things	Avoiding conflicts? Which conflicts? With whom?
Working without a plan and without priorities	Don't have to worry about priorities? Not knowing my goal?
Unplanned meetings, meetings, and conferences	Feel important? What am I avoiding with this preoccupation?
Disorder	Don't need discipline? Wordlessly expressing that I am not well?
Not completing tasks	Show how busy I am?
...	...

Today we are dealing with the problem of lack of concentration or lack of focus. This problem is widespread and a sign of a lack of prioritization. It is often better and more productive to do nothing than to do the wrong thing (e.g., "Before I do nothing, I'm going to check my email"). Because doing nothing gives you time to think and feel *what* you actually want to or should do. If you start right away with the first task you encounter, you'll soon be so busy that you won't even ask yourself whether what you're doing is relevant to you at all.

Second part of your task:

Make the following rules your own:

1. Before you start your (working) day, make a note of one to three things you want to accomplish today (not just start!), something that makes you feel you've done something useful. If you manage to do only one thing today — what would it be to make the day feel rewarding and productive?

2. Choose the highest priority task from the list of three. When in doubt, always choose the most unpleasant task to quickly get it off the table so that it no longer burdens you.

3. Put all distractions away (mobile phone to flight mode, phone to silent or answering machine, switch off computer alerts, etc.), as you learned in the last few days to work in a focused and uninterrupted manner.

Now set the shortest deadline possible (maximum 1.5 hours) and set an alarm clock for it (e.g., the timer on your smartphone, an alarm clock, an egg timer, or a timer on the web at www.how-employees-startup.com/timer). If the task definitely takes more than 1.5 hours, define the first step. This should get you as close as possible to achieving the goal in less than 1.5 hours of focused work.

Now work only on this one target until the alarm clock signals.

If you finish before the time runs out (which happens quite often), take a short break, get up, maybe get a glass of water or look out the window a bit. After a few minutes, return to your work and proceed to the next item on your list. Set a fixed time again, set your alarm clock, but make sure you don't work more than 1.5 hours without taking a break of 10 to 15 minutes.

The 1.5 hours is a guideline. Maybe it feels better for you to work a maximum of 45 or 60 minutes at a time and then take a short break. Determine your "attention span" by observing the next time you lose concentration. The same applies to short and long breaks. These should do you and your body good. So, enjoy the break and switch off, don't use it to "just do something or check your emails!"

Important: From this point forward, follow this procedure every working day. You can't manage this? Then forget about self-employment!

Why this exercise? This structure fosters focus by eliminating the impulse to start (too many) new tasks without completing the others. You need this quality to become independent successfully and to manage your life without burning the candles at both ends.

Day 18 — Tame your perfectionism

5 min.	30 min.	www.hes90.com/18	

Perfectionism is a double-edged sword: On the one hand, it helps achieve a goal with mastery. For example, one is undoubtedly grateful when the doctor performs perfectly during heart surgery. But perfectionism can also prevent you from completing something in the first place and/or lead you to neglect other things that are also important.

Therefore, the art is to carefully calculate where top performance is truly worthwhile and necessary and where "good enough" is sufficient. I maintain that "good enough" is sufficient in 95% of cases, even if we sometimes refuse to admit it.

To become more productive, the 80/20 principle described in Chapter 6 yields the most significant leverage: According to this principle, 80% of a result can be achieved with just 20% of the funds. This can be used effectively to counteract excessive perfectionism. Take planning for a wedding dinner. Two hours of planning (= 20%) will be only slightly less "perfect" than if you invest ten hours (= 100%). On the other hand, you can use the "saved" eight hours to do many other things that are also important (e.g., select wedding invitations and then decide after only 20% search time to turn your attention to other things).

If perfectionism is not an issue for you, you have the day off.

Even if you don't feel like a perfectionist, but you've been told repeatedly that you are extremely thorough or even obsessive, consider yourself a perfectionist. This lack of recognition is akin to not perceiving your strengths yourself because they seem so natural to you.

Your task for today:

Reflect on the areas in which you would like to do things perfectly in the past and in which you could achieve an equally good result in the future with considerably less effort, energy, or time. Then, for an area of your choice, decide to "take it easy" and be satisfied with "good enough." Ideally, find something to practice on today. Otherwise, note it in your calendar when you have a task where you can practice the 80/20 principle.

You will employ this principle — good enough is sufficient — in your business, when providing pragmatic and creative solutions to make your customers happy. You will not have the time or the energy to do *everything* perfectly. It's enough to focus on the very few things that your customers really care about.

Perhaps you place a lot of value in doing certain things just so. Like most of us, check whether you have "built" too many things into your life where perfectionism creates stress. That's an indicator that it's time to separate yourself from things that you've packed into your daily life over the years. Don't worry! You'll be given a task for that tomorrow.

Day 19 — Simplify your daily life

10 min.	50 min. + times in the future	www.hes90.com/19

Today is about simplifying and purifying your life. Maybe you know books like *Simplify Your Life!* or Marie Kondo's advice on organizing? If not, why not go to your favorite bookstore and leaf through these books?

In our household, daily life, circle of friends, and our subconscious, we've noted things we wanted to have, found, or were given to us. Some of them have given us joy for a long time, and some of them have annoyed us. Take advantage of the 90-Day Program to clean up and muck out this area of your life. Minimize, purge, and release irrelevant things from your life.

Your task today consists of three steps:

1. Make a list of items, tasks, activities, and people that cost you time, money, energy, and/or attention, which don't please you. Giving up, letting go, or quitting such things is good for you and gives you more freedom for your plans.

2. Prioritize your list in descending order by writing a number beside each point.

3. Afterward, record the first step to eliminate each point from your life and enter this step in your calendar. You should plan three of them in the next five working days and the rest in the subsequent three weeks. Start with the point that would give you the most "free space" or "leeway" if you eliminated it, then the one with the second most benefit if you gave it up, etc.

Here are some examples to inspire you:

- **Cancel memberships that no longer mean anything to you.** If there are things you have committed to (e.g., a club), which are no longer meaningful, and may even burden you, terminate them. Do it even if it's difficult because you're supposedly disappointing other people (e.g., club members). It will give you a stronger feeling of freedom and self-determination.

- **Think about the people you spend time with and their effect on you.** Friends are very important for happiness and health, so cultivate your good friendships; don't sacrifice them for work. But often, people have crept into your life, robbing you of energy, burdening you, and always leaving you with a bad feeling after interacting with them. Even if it takes a lot of effort: Separate yourself from them and use the time for yourself or for people who are good for you. These "energy suckers" often make you feel responsible for them or make you feel guilty when you turn them down. Don't let this put you off. It will do you good and give you more self-confidence if you decide for yourself and your life who you spend your time with.

- **Hand in tasks that are not close to your heart.** Think about what tasks and work you do in your everyday life and whether someone else can take over. For example, you could carpool with other parents to take the children to school or sports. Hire a cleaner. Maybe other people enjoy the work you have to do (e.g., gardening) or who will do it for a small wage (e.g., young people in the neighborhood). Be creative and dare to ask for help. It works better than you think!

- **Clean out your rooms, drawers, cupboards, tables, etc.** That frees you up immensely. To do this, start with just one area (e.g., the wardrobe, the bathroom, the cellar), get three large empty boxes, and set a time window of 60 minutes. During this time, go through all the things, considering whether you'll enjoy looking at them. If so, put them in the "Keep" box; if not, put them in the "Dispose of" box. If you can't decide, put them in the "Let's see" box. After 60 minutes, put the "keep" things in their place and get rid of the things in the "Dispose" box: parts go in the rubbish, the rest go on the street for others to enjoy. Throw away anything left after 48 hours. Is that a waste of resources? Yes, it is! But it's also a waste of resources if you burden your life with it, so let's close our eyes and just throw it away if no one wants it even for free.

Day 20 — Address unpleasant issues immediately

| | 5 min. | | 30 min. + times in the next four weeks | | www.hes90.com/20 | |

The description of today's task is short, but the principle behind it is essential to successfully implement your business idea later on: Get used to tackling the most unpleasant task first thing in the morning.

This gives you a good feeling for the rest of the day and dispels the bad conscience that would otherwise burden you all day long because of the unfinished task.

Now here comes your task:

Today, write down the five most important things in your notebook that you should do but have been putting off for a while. Typical examples are: Do your tax return, cancel unnecessary contracts or switch to a better provider, make a long-overdue dentist appointment, take something defective to be repaired, have a clarifying conversation, etc.

Second part of the task:

Now choose a task that you can do *today* and enter the remaining tasks as a to-do in your calendar for the next 21 days.

Afterward, sit down to the task you have set yourself for today. In the following days, complete the remaining procrastination tasks before starting any other daily or work task that day.

This exercise prepares you for future independence. You'll always have to get unpleasant things off the table quickly to a) be more satisfied with yourself and b) concentrate on the satisfaction of your customers. You will also have more energy when you have finally emptied your rucksack of unfinished business. You will need this energy in the coming weeks to implement your business idea!

Day 21 — Concentrate on the essentials

	10 min.		30 min.		www.hes90.com/21	

To achieve more satisfaction, it makes sense to assess how much trouble or joy things in your life actually cause you. Here too, the 80/20 principle has proven its worth. According to this principle, 80% of your joy results from only 20% of things in your life. Simultaneously, you can reduce 80% of your anger by changing or eliminating only 20% of your things.

Note: 20% of customers generate 80% of sales. This insight is always sobering and extremely helpful: If you significantly reduce the energy and resources you have put into the remaining 80% and invest in the 20% of top customers, you will generate substantially more turnover with much less work. Also, it is often the smaller customers who cause disproportionately more toil and trouble.

Here are a few examples:

▶ **20% of the products are responsible for 80% of sales.** Here, too, it's worth taking a closer look to see if the product portfolio can be significantly streamlined so that you can then concentrate on more profitable products. This reduces complexity — both for the supplier and for the customer.

▶ **20% of the employees are responsible for 80% of the result.** Everyone who works in a large company knows this experience. There are often a few who perform disproportionately well and many who more or less serve their time.

▶ **There are countless other examples:** 20% of the shares in a portfolio are responsible for 80% of the return; 20% of cities have 80% of the total population as inhabitants, etc.

So, and now we come to your task for today:

Sit down and think about the areas of your life where you can apply the 20/80 rule. Where does a small part of things make up a large part of the value for you? Perhaps it's a small number of friends who really give you a lot of pleasure? It's a small number of things you buy that make up the largest part of your satisfaction through consumption?

Write these points in your notebook. Then, investigate what you could do to focus only on the 20% that provides 80% of the benefit, leaving out the rest if necessary.

The second part of the task:

In the future, focus on the 20%. If you are doing something (e.g., writing a text, building something, keeping the flat nice, etc.) and the result feels "just about good enough," ask others for feedback and believe them when they say "yes, that's enough" or "that's good enough."

Why is this exercise important? Your goal is to work independently, be self-determined, *and* have enough time for your private life. Don't just get a (new) hamster wheel! It's key that you focus on the critical and essential things and that you are effective.

Day 22 — Manage your time with others

| | 10 min. | | 50 min. | | www.hes90.com/22 |

In the last few days, you've been taking care of your *personal* work organization. In the following days, make sure to continue to follow and maintain the new resolutions regularly. It takes some time until new habits feel "right." But it's worth it!

Today and in the next few days, it's all about improving your cooperation *with others*.

Your task for today:

Take a close look at the following time-eaters and consider which ones apply to your life and to what extent. Think about whether other things bother you in working with others and what you'd like to change.

Time-Eaters	Benefits
Appointments with friends, relatives, colleagues are not kept	Am I tolerant?
Gossip in the office, too many disturbances by visitors	Feel like I belong?
Unscheduled meetings, multiple meetings, and conferences	Feel important?
Do everything yourself	Feel irreplaceable?
Helper syndrome or "not being able to say no."	Feel important?
...	...

List the time-eaters in order — the most prominent first — and write them down in your notebook. Where do you feel that you waste the most time? What benefits you? And what would you like to eliminate or reduce? Do this before you continue reading.

Second part of the task:

At each point, think about how you'd like to handle it better in the future and what you can do to lose less time and be more focused. Write your ideas into you notebook.

Do this again before you read on.

Third part of the task:

Below, you will find suggestions to complement your own ideas. Which of these appeals to you? Complete your notes.

Time-Eaters	Solutions
Appointments of friends, relatives, colleagues are not kept	Immediately add an appointment to the calendar and invite others by email; give feedback when people are late, as often many people are waiting in the meeting
Gossip in the office, too many disturbances by visitors	Be obligatory when working in a concentrated manner and when visiting people, do not ask, "Hello, how are you?" but "Hello, what can I do for you?" and make it clear that you are "in the middle of something" and will get back to you later; use a "Do not disturb" sign
Unscheduled meetings, meetings, and conferences	Stay as far away from meetings as possible; ask for clear objectives and agenda or send them out beforehand; set a strong moderator; time-boxing (announce the time window for the meeting and for each topic at the beginning); say goodbye to ineffective meetings early with reasons
Do everything yourself	Learn how to delegate, even with small household tasks; ask others for help; if you have new tasks, first find out whether you are really the right person for them: if so, find someone who has already done this and use their experience
Helper syndrome or "not being able to say no."	Realize that every "yes" means a "no" to something else. And every "no" to someone else is a "yes" to your life.

Last part of the task:

Choose at least one thing that you can do today and preferably right away (e.g., draw a "Do not disturb" door sign to clearly show your family that you want to concentrate on your work).

This exercise prepares you to work with others to make your dream job a reality. For this, you will need the support and cooperation of customers, partners, colleagues, suppliers, authorities, etc.

Day 23 — Create order in the workplace

| | 5 min. | | 30 min. | | www.hes90.com/23 | |

Today, you will be able to get your workplace at home or in the office looking its best so that you have a positive and supportive working environment. The outside influences our inside and vice versa; your surroundings reflect the order in your head and in your life. If chaos reigns around you, your working day will not flow as smoothly as it should — and vice versa.

Your task for today:

Clean up your workplace today! First of all, take 60 minutes to clear the room without disturbance and set an alarm clock. Dispose of all things that you don't need or are broken. Find a permanent place for each item. Go through your pens and throw away all those that no longer work 100% well. Make a list of items you need to better organize your workplace (binders, filing trays, hole punches, staplers, paper clips, etc.).

I recommend you hang a whiteboard on the wall or buy a flipchart with a stand. It helps a lot to write things on the wall while standing and make little sketches of ideas to get creative and structure your thoughts.

Your task for the future:

From now on, clean up your workplace at the end of each working day and prepare the things you will need the next day. Write down the most important task for the next day, which — if this is the *only* thing you do — will make the next day a successful one. Plan on 15 minutes of your working time for cleaning up. So, if you want to finish at 6:00 pm, your work ends at 5:45 pm, and the remaining minutes you tidy up. For this, enter a daily recurring appointment with a reminder in your calendar.

Once a month, plan one hour before the end of work in your calendar (e.g., every last Friday of the month) to muck out, replenish supplies, prioritize filing, etc.

This exercise helps you to significantly improve your productivity, focus, and motivation at your workplace. You will need this for the next few weeks to successfully achieve your goal.

Day 24 — Request to home office

| 👤 15 min. | 📋 15 min. | 🌐 www.hes90.com/24 |

Today's task is only relevant for you if you work in an office. If this is not the case, then you have today off.

Many people find that they are much more effective and efficient when they are not working at their workplace (e.g., during a long train journey or in the home office during the Covid era). When you are not at your workplace, you automatically escape from many timewasters and often concentrate better (assuming a good working environment).

So, if it's even remotely possible for you to work partly from home (or in a co-working space), you should try to negotiate a home office arrangement with your employer for one or more days. Due to the many positive experiences on the employee and employer side during the Covid pandemic, today's chances are very good. Not only will you soon be able to do more of your work in less time, but you will also have more time to work on your own business idea.

By now, your supervisor and colleagues should have noticed how much more efficient and effective you've become due to the third week's activities. This will give you the perfect basis for argumentation to take the next step: Apply for a home office!

So, if a home office arrangement is possible for your work, you will start getting one today.

Your task for today:

Plan a day today where you take your work material (laptop, documents, etc.) home the day before and tell your boss and colleagues that you have to work from home. This can also be tomorrow or the day after tomorrow.

On this day, work in a particularly focused way and try to get as much done as possible. Write emails — of course only where it makes sense in terms of content — to show what you've done (yes, you may write emails all day long, only check your emails as usual at 11:00 and 4:00).

In doing so, you are pursuing two goals:

1. You'll discover what you still need or have to adapt to work optimally from home.

2. You'll collect documents for your boss that show how much more productive you can be from home.

Afterward, summarize your home office experiment's positive results on one page and then arrange a meeting with your supervisor. Explain to him that you have noticed how much more productive you are for the company when you work from home two days a week and that working with colleagues works just as well.

Ask your boss to try this for two weeks with the promise to stop the trial immediately if it doesn't bring the expected benefits to the company and to discuss the experience *at the latest* after the two weeks before deciding on further action. By the way, the suggestion "let's try it for a few days and then decide together whether it makes sense" often works.

If you have permission to stay in your home office for a trial period, make sure that these are the most productive days ever. That way, you will convince your supervisor and gain a little more freedom. Then gradually try to expand the proportion of home officing.

Day 25 — Set priorities and complete tasks

| | 5 min. | | 30 min. | | www.hes90.com/25 | |

Few people consciously take the time to prioritize their tasks. Therefore, they tinker with all sorts of things, feel busy, or even overloaded, without achieving great results.

If you do not prioritize yourself, the environment will prioritize for you and use you to do the things that scream "Here!" the loudest. And these are usually not the things that help you achieve your goals and feel good.

First of all, remember that *being busy* has nothing to do with *being effective. On the* contrary, it may very well be that six hours of thinking about what you really need to do, followed by two hours of work, is ten times more effective than your typical eight-hour day of busy-ness.

Start prioritizing your tasks from today and start right now.

Your task for today:

Create an overview of all the topics that are currently on your mind (e.g., developing a new business, household, children, filing, club, etc.) Now give each topic 0 to 3 points for their respective importance and urgency for you and your life and write them down for each topic (3 points = very important/urgent, 0 points = unimportant/non-urgent).

Now, draw a 2x2 matrix, as shown in Figure 101 in your notebook, and enter the topics in the appropriate place in the matrix:

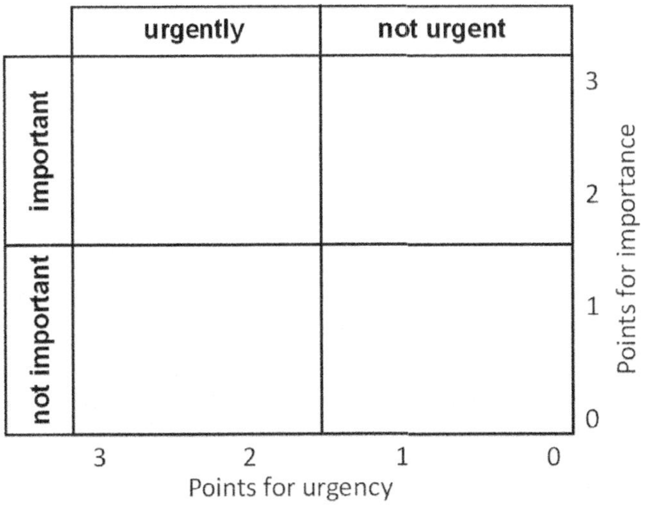

Figure 10: 2x2 matrix to classify tasks by urgency and importance

The matrix now shows the prioritization for your tasks (see also Figure 11):

I.   **Important and urgent:** *Do it yourself immediately* and avoid such situations in the future as far as possible by paying more attention to and scheduling category II tasks.

II.   **Important, but not urgent:** *Schedule* these tasks in the calendar *and complete them yourself.* For a more relaxed and successful life, you should spend most of your time here.

III. **Urgent, but not important:** Try to *delegate* these tasks to others as much as possible to relieve yourself. If they don't do it well enough, no harm done.

IV.   **Neither urgent nor important:** *Do not deal with* this task *at all* and ignore it in the future.

	urgently	**not urgent**
important	**I. Do it immediately** • Crises • Emergencies • Deadlines with high importance	**II. planning** • Planning • Prevention • Relations • Trends • Further education
not important	**III. delegate** • Meetings • E-mails • Interruptions • Calls	**IV. Ignore** • Trivial routines • Distractions

Figure 11: Decision matrix for upcoming tasks

Set yourself a tight timeframe for the prioritized tasks in which you concentrate only on these tasks.

Pack similar tasks together once a day (e.g., answering emails), once a week (e.g., processing mail and filing), or once a month (e.g., paying bills) to save time. Until then, collect all similar tasks in a fixed location (e.g., email folder, invoice compartment on the shelf) without processing them further.

What is the purpose of this exercise? You need to learn how to *not* do things and to endure it. Here the principle applies: Leave small things unfinished or even fail to successfully accomplish the big things that are important to you. You cannot and should not please everybody!

Day 26 — Leave your comfort zone: Addressing strangers

5 min.	15 min.	www.hes90.com/26	

If you want to set up your own business, it's important to gain feedback from others and formulate what you want from them. This takes courage and some practice, and that's precisely what we're working on now.

Your task for today:

Choose an event you can go to in the next seven days. And go alone! Understand this — don't take anyone else with you. Register — if necessary — for this event and add it to your calendar.

Voluntarily put yourself in a situation where you don't know anyone else. Without someone to engage with, you're more likely to interact with others. But don't put too much pressure on yourself. If you don't talk to someone right away, that's fine! Remember: everyone feels the same way you do.

Most people are happy when they are approached in a friendly manner, especially when asked for advice. Start your exercise by asking people for directions twice on the way to the event, even if you actually know the way. It is all about the exercise. You've been out and about and among strangers — perhaps, something you've never done before.

Look around for events in your city where you can meet and talk to others (art shows, book readings, music concerts, etc.). A museum is ideal. Look at the objects or works of art and simply talk to someone else who is looking at the same thing by saying what you notice or like. Just try it! And let yourself be surprised at what interesting conversations will result. And who knows — maybe this program will not only help you get your dream job in the end but you'll make meaningful connections?

This exercise prepares you to test your business idea on potential customers later on, which you also have to address.

> **NOTE:** In six days, you'll want to have a sparring partner for task 31. I'm notifying you today so that you can make an appointment with them for day 31.

Step 3:
Discover your business idea

Day 27 — Determine your target income

20 min.	90 min.	www.hes90.com/27	

Money is important. And more money makes you happier, but only up to a certain income level, as various studies have shown[26]. Even lottery millionaires are *similarly happy* or *even unhappier* after a year than before the "big win."

We should have an amount of money that enables us not to worry too much. At the same time, we should not have so much money that we have to worry about it.

So, it's helpful to know how much money you need for yourself and your family to be happy. Because going forward, you are carving out time for the important things and not simply increasing your income even more.

Jean-Jacques Rousseau (1712-1778), the French writer and philosopher during the Enlightenment period, said it succinctly and eloquently: *"The money you own is the means to freedom, the one you chase, the means to servitude."*

Here is your task for today:

Write down in your notebook, which purchases you'd like to make in your life and approximately when. First, concentrate on the absolutely necessary ones. Maybe you want to save up for a home of your own. Then think about how much money you'll need to take out a mortgage and, if necessary, to save money for a down payment. Divide the down payment amount by the number of months remaining until the planned purchase date.

SAMPLE CALCULATION FOR PLANNED PROPERTY ACQUISITION

Today's date:	November 2020
Planned purchase date:	June 2025
Estimated purchase price:	$250,000 (of which $50,000 down payment)
Time Nov. 2020 to June 2025:	54 months
Monthly required savings rate for the down payment:	$50,000 / 54 = $926/month

At an interest rate of 1.5% after purchase, the loan is due for $750 per month, to be earned from July 2026 and paid off for 27 years.

Calculate the amount of money you need for all your other plans (e.g., buying a car, costs of educating children, etc.) and add up your daily expenses. The sum is the net income you need to earn per month for the life of your choice.

SAMPLE CALCULATION FOR CHILDREN'S EDUCATION

Today's date:	March 2020
Planned start of training:	September 2032
Budget required:	$50,000 (adjusted for inflation)
Period March 2020 to Sept. 2032:	151 months

Monthly necessary savings rate for training = $50,000/151 = $331/month

TIP: As a self-employed person, you have to keep an eye on many costs that you have little or no need to worry about as an employee.

- ⊘ You bear the financial risk on your own, and you have to insure yourself, i.e., take care of health, pension, care, and social security contributions.

- ⊘ The minimum contribution to voluntary, statutory health insurance is high, and private health insurance quickly becomes expensive in old age or with family. In addition, you often have to advance medical costs, which puts a strain on your cash flow.

- ⊘ One of the most common stumbling blocks for the self-employed is a tax payment that often comes years later and is much higher than expected. A critical tip: set up your own bank account for tax payments, into which you always pay 30% of your roughly estimated profit. You should also report any drop-in profits directly to the tax office, as the tax authorities will calculate your tax burden based on your profits in recent years.

SAMPLE CALCULATION FOR LIVING EXPENSES

	per month
Housing costs (monthly rent, utilities)	$1200
Food (e.g., food, drinks, hygiene/beauty products)	$500
Clothing	$100
Transportation (car costs, public transport tickets, airfare)	$450
Education (training and study fees, material costs)	
Vacation (approx. 2,400 USD per year)	$200
Sports and leisure (gym, streaming services, theatre)	$20
Medical Expenses	$200
Other (telephone, internet, mobile phone, etc.)	$80
Cost of living	$1900
Insurance	$20
Reserves for education of children	$331
401(k)/Retirement provision	$240
Savings	$93
Installments for existing loans (student)	
Reserves for real estate	$926
Costs for the future	$1600
Necessary net income	$3500
Net income of spouse	$1950
Necessary income from self-employment	$1550

After you have made the calculation: Is it about as much as you earn (net) per month today? It's probably more rather than less. This means that your previous income is insufficient for your desired lifestyle and that you'll either have to earn more net income than today or financially adjust your desired lifestyle.

If it is substantially more, first check whether your plans are essential at the planned level and in the near future. You should have a realistic income target so that you don't raise the bar for your independence too high. Remember that your income can increase in the next few years if you are enthusiastic about a job and your business grows. If you are not in a high-paying job and your previous income has been sufficient for your life, aim for a similar income for the next two or three years.

If you are in a well-paid job today — one that demands long days, weekend work, loads of responsibility *and* stress — consider an acceptable and feasible lower income amount given significantly decreased burden, stress, responsibility, and health risks.

Wrap your head around the *value* of having more time for your family, yourself, and your hobbies. What does it mean to you? What is it worth? Everything in life has a price. You've already established the costs associated with your high income. So, eliminating those costs means paying the price of a lower income.

Suppose this isn't possible because you have so many financial obligations. In that case, I strongly recommend first establishing whether you cannot and do not want to reduce them, for example, by selling property to pay off debts. Even if this change's cost means financial loss, no money in the world can outweigh your health and your lifetime experiences.

How much money do you need per day? To calculate the number of actual working days per year as a self-employed person, we have to deduct — depending on your business model — holidays, continuing education, holidays, sick days, etc.

Let's assume that of the 365 days; you don't work on weekends (104 days), public holidays (between nine and 16 days), holidays (25 to 30 days), in case of illness (about five days), and for continuing education (about five days). That leaves 211 days per year or, on average, 17.5 days per month.

That results in a required daily net income of:

$1550 ÷ 17.5 ≈ $89 /day

Now increase the amount by your average tax rate to calculate your necessary gross income:

Gross income = net income x (1 + tax rate in percent ÷ 100)

EXAMPLE OF REQUIRED NET INCOME (AT A TAX RATE OF 45 %):

per year	12 x 1550 x 1.45	= $26,970
per month	1550 x 1.45	= $2247.50
per day	89 x 1.45	= $129.05
per hour	129.05 ÷ 4	= $32.14 (for four hours/working day)

With this exercise, you now know how much money your business idea has to yield per hour, per working day, per month, and per year. This is critical information for many future decisions and for your business model, which you will soon develop in the 90-Day Program.

Day 28 — Define when and where you want to work

👤 15 min.	📋 45 min.	🌐 www.hes90.com/28

Today's task is about flexibility. Ideally, when, where, and how would you like to work in the future? Consider four areas: your workplace, your flexibility in terms of time and space, your working hours, and your willingness to travel.

Here is your task:

Read the explanations for all four areas and fill in the tables provided for you.

1. **Work location and spatial flexibility**

   A decisive factor for your business idea is where you want to work. If, for example, you need to work where you live, you'll be more restricted than if you're willing to commute or even move.

   Think carefully about what's important to you at your place of work. Are you prepared to commute? Is it important for you to meet other people at work or is the home office more attractive to you? Would you like to work in an office or preferably outside? Would you like to be in one place all the time or do you prefer to be able to travel for your job? Should this be within your country of residence, or do you prefer to travel abroad?

   Use the table below to discover the degree of spatial flexibility you'd like for yourself:

Spatial flexibility when working	
none	bound to one place, no possibility for travel
low	tied to one place, with the potential for travel
medium	bound to a region and conditionally willing to travel
high	bound to a region and very willing to travel
very high	not regionally bound

2. **Working hours and time flexibility**

   What are your firm commitments? As a single person, you have more freedom than if you're supporting a family with several children. You may also be tied down because you have family to care for or other obligations you don't want to give up. These obligations place demands on your time flexibility (e.g., to be there at short notice for a sick child) or the possibility of working from home (e.g., to care for a parent).

Use the following table to estimate your time flexibility needs. Keep in mind that we consider the hours left for work if you have already quit your old job, i.e., you are only working independently!

Time flexibility for working	
none	< 15 hours and fixed working hours
low	< 15 hours but flexible working hours
medium	15-30 hours and fixed working hours
high	15-30 hours and flexible working hours
very high	> 30 hours

When would be a good time for you to work, and how many hours would you like to devote to work? If you want to look after your children after returning from daycare or school, your potential working hours are probably limited to four to five hours in the morning and sometime in the evening. Think about how many hours you'd like to work per day or week, minimum, and maximum. Use the following table, which you can also find at www.how-employees-startup.com/hours-table.

Example of a weekly working time budget:

	Monday	Tuesday	Wednesday	Thursday	Friday	Weekend
In the morning	3	4	3	4	3	
Afternoon	2		2			
Evening						
Total	5	4	5	4	3	
	Working week: 21 hours					

3. Travel

Some people want to escape their jobs to have time for long journeys. They dream of living in a completely different part of the world for half a year or a whole year and getting to know the country and its people. There are business ideas for self-employed people for this as well. So, if you want to be one of the globetrotters who lead a relaxed life in Asia, South America, or anywhere else in the world, this is one of the major constraints for your business idea.

Travel needs	Meaning
no professional travel	none
occasional business trips	medium
work independent of location	high

Today's task has provided more clarity about the conditional framework of your independence. Your next task will take a deep dive into details about how you want to work in the future.

Day 29 — Determine how you want to work

👤 5 min.	📋 40 min.	🌐 www.hes90.com/29

Today we'll further narrow down the areas in which you'd like to work. For example, do you like to work alone, or do you prefer working on a team? Is it important for you to interact with customers, or do you prefer to work in the background? The following table will help you answer these questions.

Now here is your task:

Go through the table from left to right and look for one or two terms in each column you like most. This will result in the following work areas, for example:

EXAMPLE: "I would like to cook (= activity from your 'dream life' of Day 9) and deliver high-quality (= segment) soups in my city from home (= where) for private customers (= for whom).

Where?	With who?	For whom?	Segment?	What?
at home	alone	Private customers	free of charge	
outdoors	as a team	Business customers	cheap	
in the office	Patients		medium price	
in the shop	Customers		exclusively	
on the computer	Partners			
on the phone	Company			
on the road	Individuals			
in my city	Animals			
in my region	other			
in my country				
worldwide				
elsewhere if necessary				

(What? column:) "dream life" from the exercise of Day 9. Here is the content of your calling: your

With this exercise, you have further narrowed down and specified the framework of your business idea.

The following steps are about validating that the idea not only appeals to you but also to your customers. This process will teach you a lot about customers' needs so that you can gradually modify your idea to maximize the probability of success.

Day 30 — Prepare the Extended Canvas

2 min.   45 min.   www.hes90.com/30

Your task today is simple and serves as preparation for the subsequent days:

Print out the Extended Canvas in large format (large poster size) in a copy shop in triplicate under www.how-employees-startup.com/canvas. Hang one copy in a convenient spot on a wall in your office. You'll glue and label Post-its there and rehang or revise them over and over again. So, make sure that you can work on the wall easily and comfortably.

Ideally, you'll want a sparring partner for tomorrow's task. Remind them again that tomorrow is the day to start.

Day 31 — Determine your target customers

10 min.	90 min.	www.hes90.com/31	

Today and in subsequent days, you'll fill in the individual fields of the Extended Canvas step-by-step. Today, you'll start with your "target group." Keep in mind that the customers who'll buy your product ("buyers") are not always the ones who use it ("users"). However, both are equally relevant for developing a successful offer. Customers and users can be the same person, especially in the consumer space, but they don't have to be, especially if you want to do business with companies or institutions.

And here comes your task:

Think — preferably with your sparring partner — who exactly are your future customers and users:

- Are they more women (e.g., yoga studio) or more men (e.g., sports bar)?

- Which age group is most interested in your offer?

- What unique characteristics does your target group have (e.g., interested in sports, health-conscious, wealthy, low income, little time, etc.)?

- In which price segment do your customers move (e.g., very cost-conscious or willing to pay premium prices for premium offers)?

Write each distinct customer segment on a Post-it without evaluation or discussion.

Once you can't think of any more customer segments, sort the customers according to their importance for your idea, possibly combine groups or divide them into subgroups. Finally, select the most important two to four customer segments and stick them in descending order of importance in the "target group" box.

It is essential for all further steps that you know your target group. If you haven't yet clearly defined and assessed your customers' needs and expectations, you won't be able to address them in a targeted manner to sell them something successfully.

Maybe you're excited that, in theory, *everyone* is a potential customer because you think you have a better chance of success. Unfortunately, it's the other way around: *If everyone is your customer, no one is your customer.* Focusing on a clearly defined niche increases the probability that your business idea will be noticed. So, instead of addressing "all mothers," it's better to focus on "working mothers with toddlers" and create a special and unique offer for them.

Second part of the task:

Try to estimate sensibly how many potential customers your target groups contain. Write your estimate [from ... to ... customers] on the respective Post-its.

Finally, take a look at your results from today. What does it look like? How does it feel? Now we have to sleep on it...

Note: If possible, it's best to make an appointment with your sparring partner again tomorrow.

Day 32 — Discover what your target customers are missing

👤 20 min.	📋 30 min.	🌐 www.hes90.com/32

A sparring partner is still helpful today, but not absolutely necessary.

After you defined your target groups yesterday, the next step is to determine what problems these people have, which ones haven't yet been solved sufficiently, and a solution for which these people are willing to pay money.

For this purpose, you should first concentrate on the target group that you consider most attractive for your self-employment.

Here is your task for today:

On more Post-its, write down your assumptions about your target group's problems, the ones you want to solve. Collect as many as possible until you can't think of anymore. Then, start to sort them by meaning and, if necessary, combine some of them to higher-level problems or divide problems into sub-problems.

The second part of the task:

At the end, select the three to five most compelling problems (from your point of view) and stick the Post-its on your Extended Canvas. Now, summarize these top problems into a general problem for the target group. Write this on a separate Post-it, which also goes as a headline in the box "Customers' Problems."

If you've identified other attractive target groups in addition to the one you identified the previous day, then apply the same process to them. The problems and needs may be slightly different for these target groups that need to be considered and addressed separately. In this way, one to three parallel business ideas will emerge, and you can decide at a later stage which ones you'd like to explore further.

Day 33 — Analyze existing solutions

| | 30 min. | | 60 min. | | www.hes90.com/33 | |

Today, you are concerned with the question of how your customers solve the problem. Despite no solution, people are still functioning, yet the problem persists. How do they do that?

Here is your task:

Research the Internet, think, ask friends and acquaintances:

- How do they deal with the problem today?
- What are the alternative solutions?
- Which competitors are active in this market?
- What prices do they charge?
- In what form can customers buy the existing solutions (e.g., one-off payment, subscription, membership, rentals, etc.)?

Write down every solution alternative, including prices and payment method on Post-its until you can't think of anymore. Now consolidate the results (you may be able to summarize some of them) and stick the best three to five solution alternatives that are available today and with which you will compete in your Extended Canvas.

Second part of today's task:

Now jump back to the "Target groups" field. Think about which subgroup in your customer segment has these problems in particular and/or is not addressed by the existing alternatives and/or is typically the first to try a new solution, even if it's not quite ready yet. These subgroups are called "early adopters" and are important for you for three reasons:

1. They are the first customers to buy, which means they generate your first income.

2. This subgroup is particularly keen to try out new and not yet finished things and to give detailed feedback. Some of these people are no longer interested in a solution once it's fully developed and a known quantity. They'd like to be the very first ones.

3. This subgroup likes to talk about the new things they're trying out, thus ensuring very credible word-of-mouth propaganda.

Getting the problems of your target customers right is a creative and iterative process. It's worth being thorough here because a well-understood and well-described problem is already half solved. There are various techniques to structure the problem description. You will apply one of them now and formulate your target customer problem hypothesis as a short, concise text.

So, here is the third and final part of today's task:

Use the prepared text at www.how-employees-startup.com/text33 or copy the following text and fill in the gaps with the results of your previous work:

For [target group] it is a constant challenge to solve the [general problem]. In each [period], these people carry out [a core activity] in order to achieve [a main objective]. This is especially true if you are a [niche].

> **EXAMPLE:** It's a constant challenge for *employees at Industrial Park X to find time for their health in addition to the stress of their job.* Every *week, the employees look for a way to do something regularly to stay healthy and productive. This is especially true if you have a family to look after in addition to your job.*

The main problem they face is the [primary functional problem related to the activity], which leads to [poor results]. Today, their best option is [substitutes], but of course, they are [the most common complaints of each substitute]. With the [main trend], the problem will only get worse over time.

> **EXAMPLE:** The main problem they face is integrating *healthy activities into their daily work routine,* which leads to *additional stress.* Today, their best option is to take care of their *health directly at the workplace by doing exercises,* but of course, *the space and time for this at the workplace* is *continuously threatened by the working day.* With the *increase in stress-related absences from work,* the problem will only get worse over time.

If there were only an easier/better/cheaper way to carry out [the core activity], customers could have [a quantifiable impact] on [their main target], leading to [positive results/emotions]. With the [number of potential customers], there is a clear opportunity to influence a large number of people in a meaningful way.

> **EXAMPLE:** If only there were an *easier* way to *integrate health activities into everyday working life*, customers could have *a measurable positive effect* on *their health and performance*, leading to *more enjoyment of life and better performance*. With a *total of 4,900 employees in Industrial Park X*, there is a clear opportunity to influence a large number of people in a meaningful way.

Here are the explanations for the terms that you insert in the blanks:

- **The target group**: Your target clients, whom you identified on the last coaching day.

- **The general problem**: What is the central problem that every customer from your target group can agree to (e.g., not enough time or money)? This follows from your summary of the problems in the first part of the task.

- **Core activity**: What do customers do while they buy and/or use your product (e.g., "book flights" or "pick up documents" or "do something for their health")?

- **Primary objective**: What is the final objective of the implementation of this activity (e.g., "Traveling abroad," or "Better health," "More enjoyment of life and performance")?

- **Niche**: Which subgroup of potential customers is most likely to be an early adopter, i.e., which subgroup wants the offer most urgently?

- **Primary functional problem**: What is the most challenging thing to do in the activity today?

- **Worst/worst results**: What is the worst-case scenario if the activity goes wrong? If the target customers are companies: What are the adverse effects on the business?

- **Substitutes**: What are the next best options or remedies available today? This follows from the third part of today's task.

- **Most frequent complaints**: Why don't customers like these substitutes?

- **Main trend**: What will increase this problem in the future?

- **Quantifiable effects**: How can the impact of solving the problem be measured?

- **Positive results and emotions**: What good things happen as a result? What is the positive business effect for B2B startups?

- **Number of potential customers**: How many people can you approach?

If you have created additional Extended Canvas's for other target groups on the previous coaching day, repeat today's step for these as well.

Day 34 — Develop a unique value proposition

👤 10 min.	📋 50 min.	🌐 www.hes90.com/34	▦

Today you will think about how you want to make your customers happy in the future. However, this is not yet about what the concrete solution looks like, but what unique value you want to create for the customer.

For example, if you are thinking about opening a yoga studio that helps stressed managers in an industrial estate to stay healthy, a value proposition might be:

EXAMPLE: YOGA STUDIO IN AN INDUSTRIAL ESTATE

Unique value proposition: **"We offer employees a space in which they can switch off from their everyday working life and center themselves to remain healthy, productive, and satisfied in the long term."**

A unique value proposition is your vision, which will guide all further activities and decisions. Don't worry if the sentence is a bit long and bumpy at the beginning. You'll refine it bit by bit because, over time, you'll continuously learn what your customers really want and what you can offer them.

Your task:

Now formulate your unique value proposition for each of your Extended Canvas variants, i.e., a simple, clear, and convincing statement of why your offer is different and worth buying. The value proposition describes the **benefit** after successfully applying your solution to the problem or the **emotional gain** that the customer or user feels and thus gets nowhere else (= "unique").

Day 35 — Work out your solution/idea

10 min.	50 min.	www.hes90.com/35	

Before you start today's task, please recall the order in which we proceeded with the development of your business idea: We first dealt with the **target customers** and then with their **problems** and previous **solution alternatives.** Then followed the **unique value proposition,** and only now — in the fourth step — is it about the solution or the core of your business idea. Intuitively, most people do it the other way around: they start with a solution idea and then think about who could use it. That increases the danger of working beyond market needs.

The critical point is that there are various possible solutions to fulfilling the unique value proposition. To illustrate this with the yoga example:

> **EXAMPLE:** The yoga value proposition can be realized, for example, by opening a high-quality yoga studio in a dense industrial area full of office workers. Classes are offered on weekday mornings, at lunchtime, and after office hours. The studio will provide small snacks and refreshments to combine pleasure (relaxation) with the practical (having a snack).
>
> But the same value proposition could also be an in-house yoga offer, where yoga teachers visit clients' office buildings to offer courses for employees at fixed times.
>
> The solution, i.e., either an owned studio or an in-house offer, solidifies the business model and clarifies how the customer benefits from the unique value proposition.

Here is your task for today:

Collect the individual aspects your solution covers on Post-its. So, what exactly does the solution consist of, what makes it stand out? Write down everything that comes to mind; you will sort it out later.

EXAMPLE OF THE YOGA STUDIO: One of many ways to design the solution includes the following points:

- ⊘ Yoga Studio
- ⊘ Dense industrial estate
- ⊘ Offers Monday to Friday, before and after office hours and during lunch breaks
- ⊘ Healthy snacks and refreshments
- ⊘ Small groups with premium quality
- ⊘ Premium Price

Second part of the task:

When you've written down all aspects of the solution, stick the four to eight most important ones as Post-its in the box marked "Solution" in order of importance. If you think of additional or new aspects over time, simply replace or add to them. The Extended Canvas is a living document, which means it's constantly being developed and updated according to what you learn. This applies to all fields, by the way.

Repeat this exercise with the other Extended Canvas if you have several alternatives.

Step 4:
Develop and test your business idea

Day 36 — Prepare the customer survey

10 min.	50 min.	www.hes90.com/36	

Before we look intensively at the next boxes in the Extended Canvas, we should check and validate the assumptions made so far. After all, what we think about are just *assumptions* about the outside world. They can be right or wrong or partially correct. Your task now is to discover this as quickly, safely, and with as little effort as possible. If the customer segment doesn't have the problem we have assumed, or our solution idea doesn't effectively solve the problem, it's a waste to think about implementing the idea further.

For this, you need courage, creativity, and chutzpah, as you'll see in a moment.

This week it's time to leave your quiet chamber, venture out into the outside world, and talk to your potential future customers! Nervous? You're right! It's challenging and nerve-racking, but it's also a lot of fun once you overcome your initial fear. And you'll be surprised how much you learn after just a few conversations.

Be prepared because many of your expectations will not be met, but keep in mind that new ideas will emerge. This is normal, and this is precisely why we're venturing forth now: To not waste another day or dollar for an idea that might not work at all!

Using the example of the yoga studio: Is a visit to a yoga studio close to the workplace an adequate solution for the relaxation, sports, and health needs of enough employees?

Since experience shows a high probability that first-round solutions won't hit the mark, we have to repeat this step several times. We must get the answer here very quickly and with little effort.

How do we check the problem-solution assumption?

That's where our 90-Day Program's segment, "Get out of the Building," comes in. It's all about getting out of the quiet little room and into the real world outside!

We refer to the risk of not having enough customers for a viable business model as **customer risk**. Four steps are necessary to eliminate this risk as much as possible.

Steps to make the customer-Eliminate risk	Example: Yoga-Studio
1. Determine which customer segment or customers have the problem. These are your target customers in the Extended Canvas.	Which people have an exceptionally high need for relaxation and recreation in their everyday working lives? For example, the employees in a dense industrial area without nature.
2. Then think: Who would be the first customers who urgently need your offer? These are the early adopters.	For example, we could target people who are interested in sports or are health-conscious anyway. Where can you meet and approach these people (e.g., in the canteen at the salad bar rather than in the smoking area)?
3. First, try to win these customers over to your offer by addressing them *directly, for* example, by addressing them personally on the street, even if this is labor- and time-intensive.	For example, you could stand at a canteen salad bar with a small yoga flyer in your hand and ask people if they are interested in a relaxation and health course. Did I mention that it takes courage and a certain amount of audacity to approach new ideas?
4. Since you can't and don't want to *directly* address all customers in the future, you must now check whether customers can also be convinced of your offer by *addressing them indirectly* (e.g., via flyers, posters, advertisements, or Google ads).	In the next step, you could, in consultation with one to three pilot companies, make a poster for the yoga class, and see how many people respond to it.

Today is the first step, and here is your task:

Think about the customers who are most affected by the problem you've formulated and where and how you can find them. Be creative and think outside the box! Where can you find them? How can you reach them? For a start, it's sufficient to be able to talk to five to eight potential customers.

Second part of the task:

Create a questionnaire on your computer that asks the following questions:

- **Description of the persons:** Do the people you've addressed really fit into the customer segment you've established? Ask about the demographic characteristics required for this (e.g., age group, profession, etc. ...). Also, prepare fields for characteristics that you don't need to query (e.g., gender).

- **Resilience of the problem you assume:** Do people actually have this problem? How stressful is it? How do they solve the problem today? What alternative solutions are they familiar with? How much money do they spend on it? etc.

- **Meaning of your value proposition:** What things come to mind when customers hear your value proposition? What about it do they find attractive? What do they miss? What do they dislike? Do they consider it credible? etc.

- **Assessment of your solution:** What does this solution sound like to the respondent? To what extent does it fulfill the value proposition? What distinguishes this solution, and what is missing? Does the solution sound better than existing alternatives? Would the solution be accepted? What price should and could such a solution be worth? How would the solution be best bought and used? etc.

Third part of your task today:

Do something different first before looking at your questionnaire again with fresh eyes a few hours later: Have you asked for all the important points? Are the questions formulated clearly and comprehensibly? Is the questionnaire short enough so that the respondents are not frustrated or overwhelmed?

Last part of your task:

Make an appointment for tomorrow or the next coaching day with two or three people you trust to test your questionnaire, ideally in person or, if necessary, by telephone or video conference.

Day 37 — Test your interview

5 min.　　　60 min.　　　www.hes90.com/37

Today you'll conduct a pre-test of your questionnaire with people from your circle of friends and acquaintances.

Here is your task:

Test your questionnaire today with two or three people you trust to ensure that it's understandable and that the survey lasts as long as you want. The survey shouldn't take longer than five to ten minutes. Improve the questionnaire today until you have a version that's *good enough* (remember the 20/80 principle). Then you're ready.

Second part of today's task:

Purchase a clipboard and good pens in an office supply store and print out 20 copies of your questionnaire because the next coaching day is the day to go! Plan how and where you'll meet potential customers and how you'll get there.

Day 38 to 40 — Meet. Your. Clients.

10 min.	120 min. (for three days)	www.hes90.com/38	

You've thought about who your customers are and where you can meet them. You also prepared your questionnaire and got some good working pens — time for some action!

Today's task will take you out of your comfort zone because very few people find it easy to talk to strangers. Fortunately, you've already practiced this in this program and are now ready!

I promise you: Once you've overcome your fear and have had your first chats, you'll notice how much fun it is and how incredibly much you'll learn. It's like any other skill: the more you do something, the better you get at it. And you'll begin to feel what it's like to be independent ...

Your task for today:

Go to where your potential customers are, take out your clipboard with the questionnaires, address the first person in a friendly and confident manner, and get going!

It's better to concentrate initially only on the questions concerning the target group and the problems rather than deal with all aspects only superficially. Therefore, at first, ask these aspects in a concentrated way and then ask if they still have time for further questions. Always ask if you can have an email and/or a phone number to ask for more information and if the person wants to be kept informed about your idea's progress. In this way, you can start to make a list of people who will be very valuable later.

You can find the necessary wording on data protection at: www.how-employees-startup.com/data-protection.

If you notice during the interview that you've forgotten certain aspects of your questionnaire, add them.

After your survey, it's best to create an Excel list or even just a tally sheet to evaluate the questionnaire's individual questions. Enter the results every evening. Only update the questionnaire if you've come up with critical new questions or if it contains gross errors.

Day 41 — Check the significance of the customer problem

⏲ 15 min.	📋 90 min.	🌐 www.hes90.com/41	▦

Last week was certainly very exciting and insightful for you, wasn't it? I hope you also had fun and felt like doing more. As a rule, the following things have happened in the last few days:

- ✓ Either you've realized that your idea is viable, but there is still some work to be done to build your existence on it. Or you've noticed that there's little or no interest, at least among the people you've interviewed so far, i.e., either you have to modify your idea, your target group, or even both.

- ✓ You've learned a lot of surprising things about your customers and your idea, which you'd never have dreamed of. That's why it's so important to go out and talk to real customers!

- ✓ You've got thoughts on how to improve your idea.

We refer to the risk of developing a product or offer that doesn't solve a relevant customer problem and is not in demand as **product risk**.

To eliminate this risk as much as possible, four steps are necessary:

Steps to minimize product risk	Yoga-Studio Example
1. We make sure that we have found a problem that's worth (money) to potential customers.	We need tangible evidence that employees long for rest, relaxation, and health and are willing to invest time and money in this.
2. Then we define the simplest solution (in the sense of being inexpensive and quick to implement ourselves) to solve the problem (on a trial basis) with real customers.	How can we simulate a yoga class near the workplace? For example, by first offering an in-house course.

173

3. We now have to apply this solution on a small scale to real customers to confirm that we have a solution that really solves the customers' problem.

We are talking to two companies and offering them a four-week yoga taster course free of charge for the employees. We put a corresponding announcement on the notice board and bring enough yoga mats for the participants.

4. Once we've shown on a small scale that we can solve real customers' problems, we have to make sure that we can do it on a large scale.

Are the participants so satisfied that they want to continue? Are they willing to pay money for it? Would they bring other colleagues? And can we implement the offer so that we can serve a larger number of customers?

Here is your task:

Answer the following questions based on the survey in your notebook:

- ◎ **How well is your business idea received?** What was particularly positive for potential customers? What did they not like so much? How did they express themselves, i.e., what words did the respondents use to describe your offer?

- ◎ **What aspects need to be improved?** What was criticized or missing?

- ◎ **Is there enough willingness to buy?** How was the price perceived? How often would customers purchase or use the offer?

- ◎ **Is the market big enough?** Are there indications that there are enough potential customers for your offer to succeed in the long term?

The next step is to gradually improve your idea. Maybe the target group is different, or you've discovered a new or different problem that's worth solving. Sometimes the target group and the problem may be appropriate, but you may have received suggestions on how to improve your value proposition and/or refine the solution.

Second part of the task:

Update your Extended Canvas according to your new knowledge, i.e., remove or add Post-its, change their order on the canvas or write what you've learned on the existing Post-its.

If you're one of the few people who hit the nail on the head at the first go, then: Congratulations!

Tomorrow, you can jump to Day 42.

Otherwise, develop your business idea based on what you've learned and repeat the steps as follows:

- If potential customers find your value proposition attractive, but the **solution is not good enough**, start again from Day 35.

- If your target group has **not** responded **positively** enough to your **value proposition**, continue with Day 34.

- If your target group **doesn't have** the **problem** you're **suggesting**, go back to Day 32.

- If you feel that you haven't found **the right target group yet**, start again on Day 31.

In your opinion, did the survey not go well at all? Then don't worry; it's more the rule than the exception at the first attempt. Sometimes the following happens: You had overlooked something serious in your idea, and it seems almost impossible to be successful with your idea, even if you would modify it significantly. If this is the case, don't give up yet! Your task then is to sleep on it for the rest of this week or a few nights. Talk to all kinds of people about your idea and the newly discovered "hurdles." Your goal is to find a way to make it work.

- If you discover an approach, start again with the changed idea on Day 31 and go through the process again (that's only two weeks).

- If you can't find a way to pursue the idea, put it down, take a two-week break, and then start a new approach on Day 31. And remember: Discovering that an idea *doesn't* work in the early stages is a good thing! With classic startup methods, you would've only noticed this after several months with a lot of invested energy in the process after your "shop" had already opened!

Day 42 — Open the channels to the target customers

	20 min.		120 min.		www.hes90.com/42

Today, turn to the next field in the Extended Canvas. It's about defining how you interact with your customers. This refers to the channels through which you interact with the customer before, during, and after the purchase:

- **Attention:** How do customers find out about your offer?
- **Evaluation:** How do you support your customers in evaluating offers?
- **Purchase:** How do you enable your customers to buy?
- **After Sales Service:** How do you support your customers after the purchase?
- **Added value**: Can you deliver added value to your customers through specific channels?

In principle, you can reach your customers through your own channels or partner channels:

- **Proprietary channels** are direct and include your internal sales team, website, emailing, or shop. Your own channels offer a higher profit margin but are usually more expensive to set up and operate. You also need experience in setting up and maintaining the channels.
- **Partner channels** are indirect and include wholesale, retail, partner websites, social networks, online advertising, posters, TV, radio, etc. Partner channels lead to lower margins but allow you to generate reach with a low initial investment and little know-how, and reach customers you could hardly reach personally with your own direct channels (think of Google advertising, for example).

Now here is your task:

Now take a pack of Post-its and ideally your sparring partner and think about the best channels through which you can best achieve the following goals, i.e., cheaply and effectively:

- **Create attention**: How can you make your offer known to potential customers? This refers to classic advertising, i.e., flyers, social media, newspapers, posters, radio, word of mouth, etc.

- **Evaluation**: How can you help your interested parties to evaluate your offer (as positively as possible)? Examples are the results of a survey, comparisons, reviews, ratings from other customers, recommendations from experts, seals of approval, awards, qualifications, etc.

- **Buy**: How do you enable your customers to buy your products as easily as possible? Examples are an online shop, retail shop, telephone, order form, self-service, etc.

- **Delivery**: How do your customers receive your service most conveniently and cost-effectively? Examples are self-collection, delivery by mail, download, in the shop, etc.

- **Service**: How do you look after your customers after the purchase? Examples are a call center, returns, in-store account managers, websites, communities, service staff, etc.

In this task, divide your channels into two phases:

Phase 1 includes the channels you'll use at the beginning to reach your customers quickly and learn as much as possible about the customers and the perception of your offer. In the beginning, what you learn about your customers and your market is much more important and valuable than sales or even profits! Here are some examples:

EXAMPLES OF THE USE OF CHANNELS FOR LEARNING IN PHASE 1:

1. For example, if you want to open a restaurant as a pure delivery service, you should deliver the food yourself in the first weeks and months to talk to your customers as much as possible. That way you can find out how they came to you, why they chose you, what they like best, what needs to be improved, etc.
2. If you want to advertise via flyers, distribute them yourself at the beginning because this way, you can directly receive feedback from your potential customers.
3. If you want to take orders, use the telephone initially, for example, so that you're in direct contact with your customers again before replacing the phone order-taking with a website with an online order form.

Phase 2 includes all the channels you want to use later when you have a good enough understanding of your business and your customers and now want to increase profitability. Now it's a matter of replacing you and finding the most cost-effective indirect channels, even if this means you lose direct contact with your customers and therefore learn fewer new things. For example, you could now hire a driver to deliver the food. Or you could pay a student to distribute the promotional flyers.

Once you've defined your preferred channels for all five areas and both phases and entered them as Post-its in your Extended Canvas, the task is complete for today! Well done!

Day 43 — Define your revenue sources

👤 15 min.	📋 45 min.	🌐 www.hes90.com/43	▦

Now it's time to get down to business: How will you earn money with your business idea in the future?

Long story short: The danger that you cannot earn enough money with your offer or that the market is too small is what we call **market risk**. To eliminate the market risk as much as possible, the following four steps are necessary:

Steps to minimize market risk

1. Identify the alternative solutions that your target customers use today to solve the problem.

Yoga-Studio Example

For example, do people use fitness studios nearby, and if so, how close are they, and how much do they cost? How long are the contracts typically for?

2. Determine the cost of the alternatives and make an initial estimate of the cost of your offer. Ask potential customers if they'd be willing to pay this price.

A fitness course costs perhaps $24 per month, and customers use it de facto only two or three times a month for 45 minutes (= $24 /2.5*75% hour = $12.5). Other yoga studios in the city center with more competition charge $15/hour. So, we assume that as an exclusive studio in the business park, we can take $20/hour and ask customers on the street for their feedback.

3. Since it doesn't cost people anything to say: "Yes, I would pay that much," we have to check — after we have determined our planned price — whether they would actually pay it. To do this, we must now present the offer very convincingly and demand a purchase decision.

Now we present our offer to the employees in one company for $20/hour, in a second company for $25/hour, and check what influence this has on the number of potential customers signing up. When we receive applications, we also ask for an assessment of how the price is perceived.

4. Once we've found a price that's acceptable to the customer, we will then gradually improve our cost structure and increase sales per customer until the business is sustainable in our view.

Suppose the yoga studio runs at $20/hour. In that case, the aim is to examine how costs can gradually be saved, for example, through cheaper advertising (e.g., customers recruit customers), higher purchasing volumes (e.g., yoga accessories). We can increase the turnover per customer by offering more courses (e.g., nutrition) or selling products (e.g., teas, yoga accessories, books)

There are basically two types of revenue sources: One-off payments (e.g., sales) and regular payments (e.g., subscriptions). **One-off payments** are relatively easy to understand and realize. **Recurring payments** are a little more complicated to plan and implement, but they have the advantage that you continuously earn money and usually plan the proceeds better.

We distinguish the following sources of revenue:

- **Selling products and services:** When you sell something, you're transferring your ownership of a physical product to a buyer (e.g., retail, hairdresser). This form of revenue stream is well known and easy to understand.

- **User fee:** This is the kind of fee you can charge as a service provider when you allow customers to use a service (e.g., car park, car-sharing).

- **Subscriptions:** If your customer wants long-term or continuous access to your products or services, they pay a subscription fee (e.g., gym membership, newspapers).

- **Rental/Leasing:** If you want your customer to have exclusive use of a product for a limited period, you can lend it, or your customer can lease it from you (e.g., rental flat, car leasing).

- **Licensing:** With licensing, you can grant others the exclusive or non-exclusive right to use your products, services, or inventions. This gives you a source of income as a rights holder without investing in production and distribution yourself (e.g., patents, franchises).

- **Intermediation fee:** If you act as an intermediary to facilitate communication and a transaction between two or more parties, you may charge an intermediation fee (e.g., dating portals, recruitment agencies, estate agents)

◉ **Advertising:** If you ensure that other companies get customers, you can charge advertising fees (e.g., internet advertising, posters).

For your business idea, think now about which of the described ways you'll earn money in the future, i.e., What will your revenue streams look like? Divide these again into two phases. First, in phase 1, i.e., in those revenue streams, which can be realized quickly and easily, and which offer you as many learning opportunities as possible? Then define which revenue streams you want to use in phase 2 in the future to make your business more profitable.

EXAMPLE: REVENUE STREAMS FOR A YOGA STUDIO

Phase 1: For a yoga studio, it's sufficient at the beginning to offer only yoga classes against **cash payment for trial lessons and 10-visit punch cards.**

Phase 2: For a yoga studio, 1-, 6- and 12-month subscriptions can be offered online and paid by PayPal or direct debit. Additional revenue streams for Phase 2 could be the sale of books and products related to yoga and possibly the rental of yoga equipment for the home.

Here is your task:

Write down the different revenue sources on Post-its and make a first estimate of how much the price could be. Use the competitors and the alternative solutions that you've already worked out on Day 33 as a guide.

Day 44 — Determine your cost structure

30 min.	90 min.	www.hes90.com/44

The cost structure describes all the costs incurred in setting up and operating your business model. This is a topic you should work on very thoroughly because a) you often overlook essential aspects during the euphoric planning phase, and b) unexpected and escalating costs are among the most common reasons for the failure of self-employment. So, go ahead and work especially meticulously here!

Your task for today:

Ask yourself the following questions and write down the answers on Post-its:

- What are the most significant cost items in my business model?
- What are the most expensive things I need to buy for my business (e.g., equipment, machinery, software, hardware)?
- What are the most expensive services or activities I need (e.g., advertising, accounting, distribution, shipping)?
- Do I have to hire people and if so, how many and for which activities?

Cost structures are more critical for some business models than for others. We distinguish between cost- and quality-oriented business models.

Cost-oriented business models focus on minimizing costs wherever possible. This approach aims to create and maintain the leanest possible cost structure, for example, through a high degree of automation and extensive outsourcing. The customer should be convinced by a particularly favorable price (e.g., Southwest Airline, ALDI).

Instead, **quality-oriented business models** focus on high quality and performance, even if this requires a higher price than other competitors. This is about premium products, personal service, boutiques, branded goods, etc. The customer should be convinced by an exceptional experience and have the feeling that they are buying something exclusive.

Both types of business model can be very successful, but only if they are fully focused on one of the two positions.

Second part of the task:

Think carefully about which segment you want to go into: As a cost leader with very lean processes and many customers with a smaller margin or a quality leader with an exquisite range of products with fewer but more solvent customers, allowing for a higher margin. Complete the Post-its in the Extended Canvas in the fields "Unique value proposition" (e.g.,"at the lowest price" or "highest quality"), "solution" as well as with your "target group" (e.g., "cost-conscious" or "demanding"), if this aspect has not yet been considered.

It's also important to distinguish between fixed and variable costs:

Fixed costs are incurred regardless of the volume of goods or services you produce. Examples are salaries, rents, and production facilities. Some companies, such as production companies, are characterized by a high proportion of fixed costs. For example, in the case of yoga studios, these include the premises, equipment, insurance, and advertising costs, regardless of how many people actually come to the yoga studio.

Variable costs are proportional to the volume of goods or services produced. In the case of a yoga studio, for example, only a few costs are variable, such as the consumables, such as tea, toilet paper, possibly the yoga teachers if they are only paid on demand, etc.

Fixed costs can also be converted into variable costs (and vice versa). For example, the yoga room could only be rented by the hour if enough participants have registered. This can be especially helpful in the initial phase when there are not many customers, and costs can be saved until the classes are regularly full enough.

Third part of the task:

Look at the cost Post-its worked out so far and sort them according to variable and fixed cost items for your business idea and mark that on the Post-it.

Then estimate or research the costs for each item on the Internet (fixed, per month, per year, or per customer) and write them on the corresponding Post-its. Now glue them in two columns for fixed and variable costs and descending by amount.

Day 45 — Calculate the revenue potential of your business idea

10 min.　　90 min.　　www.hes90.com/45

With the last two tasks, you've laid the foundation and worked out the necessary figures to make an initial calculation of the financial potential of your business idea. So, today it remains mathematical for now!

Your task for today:

Calculate in a spreadsheet (e.g., Excel, Google Sheets) the sum of fixed and variable costs, summarized by period, such as all one-off costs, all monthly costs, all annual costs, and all costs per customer. You can use the example Excel under www.how-employees-startup.com/calculation and adapt it to your needs.

Cost position	Unique	monthly	Annually	per customer/month
Room deposit	1,000			
Room rental		550		
Room service charges incl. energy		190		
Room equipment	8,000			
Yoga material			1300	
Advertising material		90		
website	2,500		500	
Consumer goods (tea, candles, ...)				3
2. yoga teacher		1,200		
Total	**11,500**	**2,030**	**1,800**	**3**

The figures can then be used to calculate the so-called **break-even point**, i.e., the point at which all your previous costs are covered, so that you start earning money from that point on (cf. Figure 12). In the yoga example, it takes twelve months until all initial and running costs are covered, and the first dollar is earned. It's not uncommon for it to take one or two years to make a profit, depending on how high the fixed costs of a business idea are.

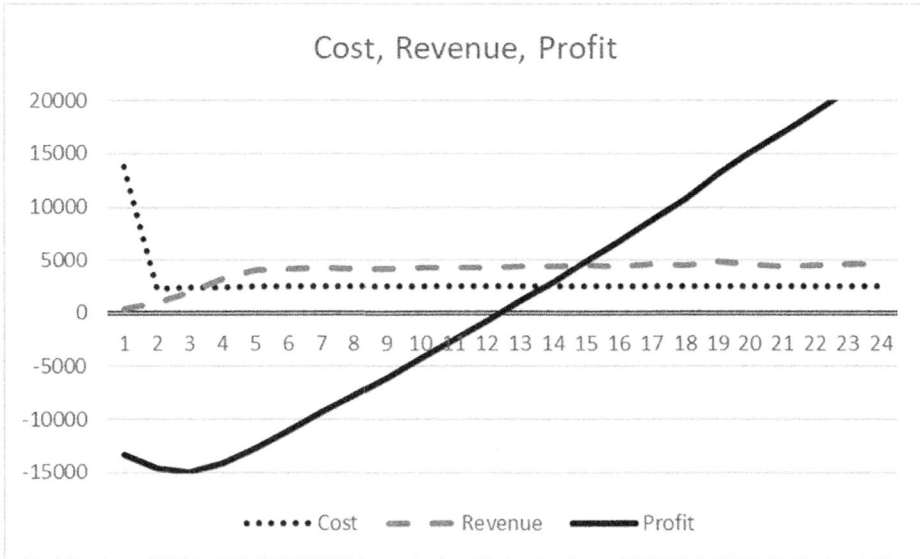

Figure 12: The course of costs, revenues, and the result in the example

Now you can also estimate pre-tax income given your assumptions are confirmed. Compare Figure 13.

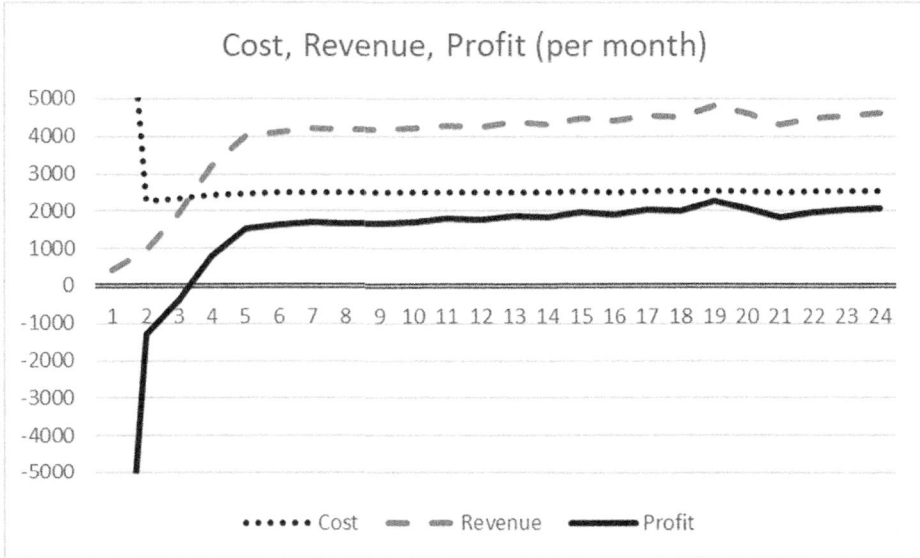

Figure 13: Result per month in the example

The monthly income before taxes in this example is around $2,000/month. Now you need to check whether this matches your expectations and needs, which you determined on Day 27. If not, you'll either have to adjust your business idea so that the income is sufficient or check whether you can get by with less.

You must have a thorough understanding of the cost/revenue relationship. Now check out what happens when the various parameters change.

Second part of the task:

Play around with the numbers a little to see how the result changes when the various influencing factors change:

- What if I only win half as many customers or 50% more than estimated?

- How does the revenue change if I increase or decrease the price of my service by 10%?

- What influence do the fixed costs have, i.e., how does the break-even point shift if I increase or reduce them by 10%, 25%, or 50%?

- What happens if I can convert fixed costs into variable costs (e.g., one-off acquisition costs through rent/leasing spread over the term; freelancers I only pay for hours worked or salaried employees with a fixed income)?

Write down the findings in your notebook — and, if necessary — on the Post-its in the Extended Canvas.

Wow! You've done quite a lot in the last three days, and for the first time, you've got a feeling for the financial potential of your idea. How does that feel?

Day 46 — Define key figures and targets for success

👤 5 min.	📋 30 min.	🌐 www.hes90.com/46	[QR code]

Today we're moving away from purely financial key figures to talk about key figures that indicate whether you're on the right track to your business idea implementation.

Here is your task for today:

In the following, I will present you with various key figures that illustrate your business idea's development. Think about the target values you need to achieve with the key figures to have a sustainable business model. In this way, you'll always know later whether you're approaching your goal as planned and if not, why not.

Write the key figures relevant to your business and your goals per key figure on a Post-it and stick them in your Extended Canvas.

Customer acquisition costs

As soon as you start making money, you have to make sure that it doesn't cost too much to attract new customers. To measure your *customer acquisition costs*, use the following formula:

$$KAK = \frac{\frac{EK}{LD} + MK + WK}{NK}$$

Where the abbreviations stand for the following:

KAK	= *customer acquisition costs*
EK	= *development costs*
LD	= *lifetime of the product in months*
MK	= *marketing costs per month*
WK	= *maintenance costs per month*
NK	= *number of new customers per month*

Before you get real data from your business, you have to estimate the various costs. In addition, use empirical values that you google on the Internet to check your estimates' plausibility.

Customer acquisition costs can change over time as you introduce new products and services, improve your processes, etc. Therefore, you must check later on whether your customer acquisition costs are within the estimated or planned range.

Customer loyalty

Customer retention is a decisive success factor, as it's much more expensive to win a new customer (customer acquisition costs) than to continue to serve an existing one. Therefore, you should measure how long customers stay with you and how often they come back. This gives you important information about the quality and uniqueness of your offer.

Viral range

The viral reach indicates how well your business model is integrated via social media such as Facebook, Instagram, LinkedIn, and Twitter. Social media is a powerful advertising channel when used properly. Unless you happen to be an expert in social media marketing yourself, you'll probably outsource this task. This is a vast field and explaining this in detail would go beyond this program's scope.

Churn rate

The churn rate indicates how quickly you lose customers. When used as an internal metric, sales must be evaluated to see if it's an expected natural part of your business or a sign of a deeper problem.

Revenue and income

Revenue is the key variable to check whether your business is thriving. Profit is the key indicator to check whether you're earning enough from your business to be able to run it sustainably. It typically takes a few months or even years until a business is big enough to not only cover the (initial) investments and running costs but also to make a profit. Therefore, it's very important to estimate and plan these key figures so that you'll notice early on if the business doesn't develop as hoped and needed.

Day 47 — Determine your core activities

| 👤 10 min. | 📋 50 min. | 🌐 www.hes90.com/47 | ▦ |

The core activities on the Extended Canvas are all business activities required for your business's success in the market. Typical business activities include product or service development, marketing, production, sales, service, and administration. The core activities naturally depend on your business idea and vary greatly.

> **EXAMPLES OF CORE ACTIVITIES**
>
> For a **yoga studio,** this includes selecting and setting up the studio, advertising, running yoga classes, and bookkeeping.
>
> For a **soup service,** this includes advertising, selection of dishes, purchase of ingredients, preparation, storage, and delivery.

That is your task for today:

Now take Post-its with two different colors and think — ideally with your sparring partner — about the tasks that need to be done to develop your business idea and run your business. Think about them until you can't think of anything else. You can also add more later.

Then evaluate the activities by their importance for success from both customer and financial perspectives. In other words: Which activities will be particularly attractive to your customers if implemented outstandingly well, and which can deter your customers if implemented poorly? In a yoga studio, the quality of the course management, the location, and atmosphere of the premises are much more important for success than the quality and efficiency of the bookkeeping.

Sort the Post-its by descending importance on your Business Model Canvas and consolidate tasks that can be summarized if necessary.

With the previous task, you should have already sufficiently mapped your business model with activities.

Second part of the task:

The next step is to examine how and where you can differentiate yourself further from your competitors to increase your chances of success.

The choice and quality of your channels and customer relations are particularly important for your competitiveness, as they link your customer segments to your value proposition.

So, take another close look at the chain "customer segment" ⇔ "channels" and "customer relations" ⇔ "value proposition", and consider which activities could play the greatest role here.

EXAMPLE: YOGA STUDIO

My customers are health-conscious employees in the industrial estate with little time [= customer segment], which I gain by addressing them personally (e.g., with a retractable banner in the foyer of the companies = channel) to establish a personal customer relationship [= customer relationship]. This enables me to implement my value proposition of making an effective and individual health offer that takes the job reality of employees into account as much as possible [= value proposition].

From this consideration, it follows that the activity "Personal Interaction" is of particular importance, not only when the yoga studio is opened but also for its continued operation. This high-touch interaction can be a decisive competitive advantage but must also be planned and paid for with time and resources when the business idea is born.

So, finally, mark on your Extended Canvas, which core activities play an outstanding role in differentiating yourself from the competition.

Day 48 — Identify your core resources

10 min.	50 min.	www.hes90.com/48	

Today it's all about what you need to implement and run your business idea. You already received important information on Day 44 when you worked out the most important cost items.

Your task today:

Take your Post-its and collect all the capital and consumer goods you need to realize your idea. This is not about every detail, but about similar classes of capital goods (e.g., "furnishings" instead of chairs, tables, and carpets) and consumer goods (e.g., "housekeeping" instead of soap, toilet paper, and bin liners).

Imagine exactly how you **build up your business idea**: what do you need to get started? Here you're more likely to find the capital goods that you need to purchase once only or purchase new ones at longer intervals.

Then imagine how you **run your business**. What tasks do you do every day, week, month, or year (see your core activities of Day 46), and what do you need to do these tasks? Here you're more likely to find the consumer goods that need to be bought regularly.

Stick the Post-its in the order of importance on the "Core Resources" field of your Business Model Canvas. Now compare the result with the contents of the cost structure. Are there things that you've not yet considered? Or do you need to adjust your cost structure with today's knowledge? Then update the relevant sections.

Day 49 — Identify your core partners

👤 10 min.	📋 50 min.	🌐 www.hes90.com/49

Having dealt with the core resources yesterday, today is about identifying the partners you need for implementation. Partners are people, companies, authorities, institutions, etc. with whom you interact sporadically or regularly to build and run your business.

Your task today:

Take your Post-its and note down all the core partners you need to implement your idea. Usually, you'll need certain service providers for the development of your business idea (e.g., designers, web programmers, interior designers, consultants) and others for the later operation.

Imagine again exactly how to **implement your business idea**: Whose help do you need to implement the core activities? What do you want to do yourself, and what can you leave to others to reach your goal faster and more professionally? If in doubt, it's better to delegate tasks because a) you'll have enough to do anyway and b) your stress level should remain at a healthy level through independence, even if this means sharing part of the income with partners. Believe me, it's usually worth it, because time on your own is the scarcest resource today, isn't it?

Then imagine how you **run your business**. What things have to be done every day, every week, or every month and whose help do you need? For example, daily cleaning, weekly website updates, monthly billing, accounting, or annual inventory.

Stick the Post-its in the order of importance on the Extended Canvas. Now compare the result with the contents of the cost structure in both the canvas and your Excel spreadsheet. Maybe the costs for some partners are not yet included? Then update the corresponding places.

Day 50 to 52 — Simulate your offer

👤 20 min.	📋 90 min.	🌐 www.hes90.com/50	[QR]

Today starts one of the most important steps for your business idea: You'll think about how to "simulate" your offer in such a way that potential customers have the impression that they can already buy it.

Key takeaway: It's critical to ensure that your offer will produce enough buyers in the market as early as possible. And the only way to find out is to force people to make a real purchase decision.

Why?

Unfortunately, it's not enough to ask people for an assessment, like: "Imagine that this product is already finished. Would you be willing to buy it, and how much would you be willing to pay?" People are usually just too nice, and many will tell you what you want to hear: "Oh yes, I can imagine buying something like that. Maybe $20?" or: "Well, why not? Sounds quite good. How much would I be willing to pay? Well, maybe $10 to $15 maximum — I'm not sure." But if they actually see your offer in the shop, without your personal approach, they'd rather spend their money on something else.

Here is a little story about it:

> **EXAMPLE:** When Sony launched the Walkman in 1979, they considered what color the device should be. They decided to do a test with potential customers and showed them the device in three colors: black, silver, and yellow. The testers were asked which one they liked best, and the majority chose the yellow device. When they left the room after the interview, they could choose a Walkman at a table as a thank you. Contrary to their own statements, a great majority decided on the black one ...

So, now your creativity, cleverness, and courage are required: What could you tell and/or show to your potential customers so that they are convinced that they can buy your product or service *now*?

FOUR EXAMPLES OF SIMULATING AN OFFER FIRST

Example 1: Culture Farm for families and people interested in culture

Tatiana had the idea of opening a "culture farm" — to convert an old farmhouse into a café with small regional vegetarian snacks, a culture room for small concerts and readings, and many play facilities for children. She wanted to manage the organization and childcare while handing over the other tasks (café operation, vegetarian food, and cultural program) to others who also wanted to become independent. Her target group is urban families with medium-to-high income and people interested in culture, for whom sustainability is important. She had already found a good location near a suitable district and wanted to check out how the target customers received the idea.

For this purpose, she had flyers designed and 500 copies printed for $100. The flyer illustrates a beautiful farm with families having a relaxed coffee and eating cake while children play in the garden. A second picture shows a concert by a trio in a cozy, intimate atmosphere with candles on the tables.

The flyer lists the five most important points: "Coffee specialties and homemade cake," "regional and fresh cuisine," "play opportunities for young and old," "colorful cultural program," "romantic farm in the middle of nature."

But the most important point is a corner of the flyer that says:

Voucher for $30 on your first visit for all food, drinks, and events.

Therefore, the flyer represents a value voucher, an opening offer at a reduced purchase price of $10.

Example 2: Yoga studio in an industrial park

To test the demand for the yoga studio, it's enough for Marie to design a nice retractable banner (approx. $50) and have it printed (approx. $40) as well as print out a few contracts.

The retractable banner is designed to show a nice picture of a yoga class in a wonderful atmosphere (approx. $10) as well as the three most important features, for example:

- Healthy & fit with only 1 hour/week
- Course times adapted to your working hours
- Located only two minutes away

The contract is only one page long and includes the most important customer data, and describes the various offers, including prices. This means that customers can already register for a course.

Marie approaches the HR departments of various companies to explain her offer. Usually, there is one person responsible for employee health programs. Marie makes an appointment with this person to clarify further details relevant to both parties.

Marie explains that she'd like to set up a small stand over a few days to explain the idea of her yoga health care to employees and to better understand their needs. So, she openly admits that she's still in the development phase and wants to make sure that the offer appeals to the employees and fits their needs. Most companies are amenable to this because they're also interested in ensuring the offer suits their employees' needs.

Example 3: Selling wool and knitting patterns for children on the Internet

Stefanie wants to turn her hobby into a profession and start a website for selling wool and knitting patterns for children on the Internet. To test the demand for knitting patterns for children and the wool that goes with them, it's sufficient for Stefanie to first set up a simple sales website (cost approx. $500), offer the first packages of patterns and wool, and run a Google Ads campaign for one week (cost approx. $200). User reaction or willingness to buy informs customer needs, which she then used to modify her offer and her advertising messages. The wool for this test phase is purchased by Stefanie only after customers have ordered; the knitting samples are printed out at the printer and sent by post.

Example 4: Pre-prototyping an invention: It can be done even earlier!

Surely, you're familiar with the term "prototype." A prototype is a thing that serves as a model for other, similar things or a preliminary copy for later mass production. Often you try to build a functional prototype of an idea with a lot of money and effort to test how it will be received.

A more radical approach is so-called pretotyping. Here, an attempt is made to simulate that the prototype can already do something, but which was not realized due to lack of money or time.

Here is an example: I wanted to develop and market a new technology that allows presentations to be controlled by gesture (e.g., "swiping the air"). To test how this idea is received by the audience, the presenter, potential customers, or even investors can use the following trick:

I invite people into a room with a projector and a screen. Then I present a small black plastic box and explain that it's a prototype of a new, revolutionary technology. I start my laptop, explain that the prototype is now connected to the laptop via Bluetooth, and start a PowerPoint presentation. Now I swipe in the air to the left and right, and indeed as if by magic, the presentation jumps back and forth, obeying my hand gestures. Then I ask an audience member to come forward and briefly teach the gestures to them. When they try it, the prototype works perfectly and obeys the spectator via hand.

Now I'm ready for feedback. What does the audience think of the presenter's hand gestures? How do I feel doing gestures in the air? Are potential customers interested in the technology? Do the investors want to invest in the idea?

When I have all my answers, I reveal the secret: The plastic box is completely empty. In fact, a colleague of mine sat in the back row and controlled the presentation with a standard beamer control so that nobody saw it. We simulated the idea together and, thanks to the plastic box on the table, gave the impression that the product was already finished.

If feedback was rather negative, we'd drop the idea altogether and have thus saved months of work and many thousands of dollars. Positive feedback would mean we'd have a higher certainty that the idea is worth investing further. Ideally, we already secured the first customers and investors who want to participate.

So, now it's your turn; here's your task:

How can your offer be presented convincingly with minimal time, effort, and money as possible? Be creative and dare to think "out of the box." This step differentiates entrepreneurs who break new ground from employees who only function within a confined space of possibilities.

Days 53 to 57 — Test your offer on real customers

10 min.	120 min. - daily for 5 days	www.hes90.com/53	

You've now had some time to make your idea so "tangible" and "experienceable" that potential customers can make a purchase decision. Now plan for the next five days when, how, and where you want to test your idea.

CONTINUATION OF THE EXAMPLES FROM DAY 50 TO 52

Example 1: Culture Farm for families and people interested in culture

Tatiana and her girlfriend venture out to chat with families and individuals in the surrounding area who they consider their target group. They explain the concept of their "Culture Farm" and invite them to drop by next weekend.

This leads to a conversation about Tatiana's idea, and she learns a lot about her target clients' interests. Finally, Tatiana asks if they would like to buy one or more "vouchers," which would save them 25%. Now they've measured how attractive their idea is. If people decide to buy and pull out their wallets, that's an excellent sign.

Now Tatiana discloses the secret, thanks the people very much, and apologizes for not being able to sell the vouchers yet because she is still in the planning stage. She wants to make sure that she has something to offer that her customers really like, so she tested whether the offer already fits. Tatiana wants to spare them, the customers, a bad experience, and the risk of a project that was built with heart and soul but failed. She thanks the customer once again for the valuable conversation and asks if she could have their email address to inform them when the "Culture Farm" actually opens. As a small thank-you and compensation, she gives a discount voucher worth $10 for the first visit.

If you talk to people in a friendly manner and honestly explain why you had to lead them on, you'll meet with goodwill and support in 99% of cases. Dealing with the remaining 1% who are annoyed is just part of doing business. Don't take it personally. You can never please everybody. But that's exactly why you've moved out of your comfort zone a few times in recent weeks. If you want to become an entrepreneur, you have to do something, and that means taking risks and being creative to achieve your goal. The important thing is that you end up being open and honest, not hurting anyone, and treating others with respect.

Yoga studio in the industrial park

As agreed, Marie now stands in the company's foyer in the morning, at lunchtime, and at the end of work with her beautiful retractable banner, a folding table, the contracts, and a few small goodies (e.g., sweets). She looks friendly and tries to interact with the employees. Marie explains her concept, answers, and asks questions about employees' interests and ends by asking if they want to register.

Here too, she reveals the secret the moment the contact person grabs the clipboard to fill out the contract. As in the previous example, she explains the background to this test and how important it is for her to build something that truly meets the interviewer's needs.

This will result in further conversation, and Marie will ask if she can just write down name and email in the contract to notify them as soon as the yoga studio opens. As a small thank you, the contact person will receive a voucher for three free yoga classes. In this way, Marie is already building up her first customer base.

Sale of wool and knitting patterns for children on the Internet

Through the Google Ads campaign, potential customers are immediately directed to the website, and Stefanie can immediately see if and how many people really want to buy her offer. Here, Stefanie has two options:

1. The website can be designed to only count when a customer clicks on the "Buy Now" button. The customer doesn't enter the payment process but sees a friendly explanation of why the offer isn't yet available. Again, it's possible to collect email addresses to inform about the real website's launch if the customer agrees.
2. She can actually complete the purchase, pack and ship the goods "by hand" as long as she has easy access to the goods (e.g., simply go to a specialist shop, buy the wool, and print the knitting pattern in the copy shop in the correct format). Of course, this process isn't yet sustainable because to make money, she has to buy larger quantities or have the goods shipped directly from another retailer ("drop shipping"). The advantage of this approach is that she can win her first (satisfied) customers. Through interaction with the customers and by manually going through the processes, she learns a lot about her business to automate and streamline it later.

So, here is your task:

In the last few days, you've worked out your precise way of simulating your offer. You know who you want to address and where you can find your target group. Now you can get out of your garage! Talk to your customers! I know that this takes some effort. But you can't get around it! If you want to do something and win (your freedom and a job that fulfills you), you also have to be daring and leave the beaten track. So, have courage! You have nothing to lose but a lot to gain! Have fun!

Days 58 to 60 — Improve your offer

| 10 min. | 90 min. | www.hes90.com/58 |

Over the past weeks, you have learned a lot about your business idea, your customers, and also about yourself.

What is the result, how do you feel? Are you euphoric because you had good conversations and people want your offer? Or are you discouraged because your expectations have not been met? Maybe you've got reverence for the next steps because you notice things are getting really serious, and your idea is slowly becoming reality.

Here is your task for the next three days:

Use the next three days to consolidate the results, update the Extended Canvas, update your calculation, and discuss the findings with a sparring partner.

As mentioned above, a business idea is constantly evolving because you validate assumptions about the customer and the market and find that minor or major corrections are needed. This is normal and a good sign!

And if you discover that your business idea just won't work, that's also a great success!

Otherwise, you would have lost a lot of time and money if you had implemented the idea using the classic method. The motto is "Fail fast!" so that if the idea was not quite the right one, you have time and resources to test the next version of your business idea or a completely new one. And if at some point, you just don't fail anymore, you've reached your goal.

I know this sounds paradoxical at first glance. But the point is to establish as early as possible whether an idea doesn't work and not to lull oneself into false hopes for a long time. Because then the "disappointment" of feeling defeated is all the more intense and expensive.

Day 61 to 65 — Set up customer channels

👤 20 min.	📋 90 min.	🌐 www.hes90.com/61	▦

If the tests of your idea were positive enough in the last few days, take the next step. If not, repeat the steps from Day 31 if you need to make fundamental changes to your idea or later, between Days 32 and 35, if you only need to make detailed changes to your business idea.

Here is the task for today and the next four days:

Expand channels leading to your target customers that you can easily tap without high investments.

The following channels are at your disposal:

Channel ++ = very high + = high 0 = medium - = low - - = very low	Purpose Advertising	Inform	Sale	Deliver	Support	Costs	Reach	Individualized
Personal approach								
Retail shop	✓	✓	✓	✓	✓	++	-	++
Field salesforce		✓	✓	✓		++	-	++
Service staff			✓		✓	++	-	++
Information stand/trade fair	✓	✓	✓		✓	+	0	++
Email	✓	✓		✓	✓	--	0	+
Telephone/Call Center		✓	✓		✓	+	0	+/0
Distribution of flyers with/without address	✓	✓				-	-	+/-
Live chat		✓			✓	-	+	0
Postal consignment/forwarding	✓	✓		✓		+	-	-
Impersonal approach								
Website	✓	✓	✓	✓	✓	+	++	-
Blog	✓	✓	(✓)		✓	--	++	-
Online marketing (e.g., Google Ads)	✓	✓				+	++	-
Social media (e.g., Facebook Ads)	✓	✓				+	+	0
Email newsletter	✓	✓		(✓)	✓	--	-	0

Info mail	✓	✓		✓		+	-	0
Flyers	✓	✓				-	-	-
Radio Advertising	✓	✓				++	+	-
Television advertising	✓	✓				++	+	-
Theater Advertising	✓	✓				+	0	-
Posters	✓	✓				+	0	-
Sponsorship	✓					+	0	-

To get started, you only need channels for advertising, information, sales, and delivery. As you can see in the table, some channels can cover all aspects (e.g., website). Usually, you'll combine different channels and later add others or "switch off" previously used channels (e.g., distributing flyers) because you want to focus on more effective ones (e.g., social media marketing).

CONTINUATION OF THE EXAMPLES OF THE USE OF CHANNELS

Example 1: Culture Farm for families and people interested in culture

After the encouraging reactions during the first tests, Tatiana had a **website** created for the Culture Farm and continues to use the channel **"display and distribute flyers"** to address her target group directly and learn more about their needs. She knows that she'll soon have to switch to more effective and more expensive channels and decides to use social media marketing.

Via **www.upwork.com,** she has found a suitable freelancer who will set up a **Facebook page** and launch **Facebook campaigns** with a regional focus. She defines a budget of $200 per month for this channel and develops effective advertising texts together with a friend.

She has found a mother of two children among her friends who would like to bake the cakes for the café to earn some extra money at home. Since this mother also likes to blog, they decided to integrate a **blog** at the Culture Farm, which the two of them would like to fill alternately with suitable content about children and healthy, tasty food. The website programmer charges $100 to integrate the blog and both reserve three hours a week to post one blog article a week.

So, to start, Tatiana uses the following channels: It's clear to see the focus of the channels is on advertising and information, the costs are still relatively low, and there's a mixture of more personal (e.g., blog) and impersonal approaches.

Channels for Culture Farm	Purpose					Features		
	Advertising	Inform	Sale	Deliver	Support	Costs	Reach	Individualized
Personal approach								
Distribution of flyers with/without address	X	X				-	-	+/-
Impersonal address								
Website	X	X	X	X	X	+	++	-
Blog	X	X	(X)		X	--	++	-
Social media (e.g., Facebook Ads)	X	X				+	+	0

Example 2: Yoga studio in an industrial estate

Marie continues to use her small stand with retractable banner, bar table, and flyers to advertise and inform interested people. She is also in the process of having a website created and is already planning to offer customers the possibility to book courses directly online. It's important to her that she tests this sales channel early on because she wants to have as little to do with money as possible in her daily teaching practice and doesn't want to talk to customers about course fees. In most companies, she is also allowed to display her flyers.

From the test phase, she has now received a quite respectable number of email addresses from interested parties. She decides to set up a newsletter to inform her clients and potential clients about interesting topics concerning yoga, health, and stress reduction. Her web programmer sets up the tool "MailChimp" for her, which is free of charge for the first 2,000 contacts. This should be enough for the start phase and testing.

As there are three very well-located poster spaces in the industrial park, she would like to use them to advertise her new yoga studio. To test the suitability, she initially rents only one poster for the shortest period (four weeks). To differentiate between the channels, she gives a slightly different website name. She has her web programmer use Google Analytics to measure how many customers come to her website via the poster.

The following table shows an overview of the selected channels. It's clear that this time, sales via two channels are already being tested.

Channels for the yoga studio	Purpose					Features		
	Advertising	Inform	Sale	Deliver	Support	Costs	Reach	Individualized
Personal approach								
Information stand/trade fair	X	X	X			+	0	++
email	X	X				--	0	+
Distribution of flyers with/without address	X	X				-	-	+/-
Impersonal address								
Website	X	X	X			+	++	-
Flyers	X	X				-	-	-
Posters	X	X				+	0	-

Example 3: Selling wool and knitting patterns for children on the Internet

Stefanie continues to use her Google Ads campaign, and has it expanded. She further developed her website based on Google Analytics findings. She invests $100 per month in Facebook Ads to test this channel and compares it with Google Ads.

Her Google Ads expert recommended maintaining a blog on her website, not dependent on paid advertising in the medium and long term, but also to get "organic traffic," i.e., visitors who come to her via a standard Google search (without advertising). She already feels like writing something from time to time but decides to ask her friends, who also like knitting, to join her.

To get more visitors to her website right from the start, she decides to write to sewing schools to draw attention to her new offer. She writes a friendly email and commissions a freelancer via www.fiverr.com to do an online search of all sewing schools for $250 and send the email on her behalf.

Channels for knitting pattern sale	Purpose					Features		
	Advertising	Inform	Sale	Deliver	Support	Costs	Reach	Individualized
Personal approach								
Email	X	X		(X)	X	--	0	+
Impersonal approach								
Website	X	X	X	X	X	+	++	-
Blog	X	X	(X)		X	--	++	-
Online marketing (e.g., Google Ads)	X	X				+	++	-
Social media (e.g., Facebook Ads)	X	X				+	+	0

Days 66 to 70 — Test your channels

5 min.   90 min.   www.hes90.com/66

Start testing the first new channels as early as possible once they're set up. Your goal is to find out how well you reach your target customers with different channels and how they react to your offer. Depending on the channel, your customers' reactions or the effect of your channels can be measured differently.

The following table provides some ideas:

Channel	Typical measurement criteria
Personal approach	People reached/hour, Interested parties/hour, Purchases/hour
Retail shop	Visitors/day, Purchases/day, Purchases/customer, Revenue/day, Revenue/customer
Field salesforce	Customer visits/week, Sales/week, Sales/customer visits, Revenue/month, Revenue/customer
Service staff	Customer visits/week, Successful service Calls/customer visits, Time/customer visit
Information stand/tradeshow	Visitors/hour, Interested parties/day, Sales/day
Email	Reactions/Total number
Telephone/Call Center	Calls/hour, Customer satisfaction, Sales/telephone calls, Resolved service requests/all requests
Distribution of flyers with/without address	Distributed flyers/hour, Conversations/distributed flyers

Live chat	Chats/hour, Customer satisfaction, Resolved service requests/all requests
Postal consignment/forwarding	Non-deliverable items/All items Returns/All shipments
Impersonal Approach	
Website	Visitors, Unique Visitors, Returning Visitors, Page Impressions/Views, Average visit duration, Bounce Rate, Conversion Rate, Return on Investment
Blog	Traffic figures (what's going on on w/my blog), user behavior (who stays where and for how long?), traffic sources (where do my readers come from?), content check (which blog posts are best received?), Social Signals (Shares, Likes und Retweets)
Online marketing (e.g., Google Ads)	See Google Analytics and Google Ads in your Google Account
Social media (e.g., Facebook Ads)	See Facebook Ads Dashboard in your Facebook account
Email newsletter	Delivery rate, opening rate, click rate, effective unique click rate, bounce rate, return on investment, double opt-in rate, reading time, unsubscribe rate, churn rate
Info mail	Response rate, cost per response, number of requests, Number of newly generated contact addresses (leads)
Flyers	Performance measurement through QR Codes, online redeemable voucher codes, own website or microsite, landing pages

Here is your task:

For each of the channels you've chosen in the last few days, define what you consider to be the two or three key figures for measuring success and note them in the Extended Canvas on the channels' Post-its.

Then create an Excel sheet and enter the key figures from now on to measure them weekly and track their development.

Days 71 to 75 — Improve service and channels

5 min.	30 min.	www.hes90.com/71	

From the tasks of the last two weeks, you can clearly see that the further we progress in the foundation process, the less specific the program can be in terms of what you should do and when. That is because it's less and less predictable in which direction your business idea will develop. It's now increasingly important that you obtain the information you need for your specific decisions yourself, or if necessary, from the Internet or specialist books.

By using new channels, you gain more expertise about your customers, your business idea, and how you present it. You'll also learn a lot about the channels themselves and how they fit in with your business idea.

Here is your task for today and the next four days:

Use the channel test findings to both develop your business idea — both on the Extended Canvas and in the measures already implemented — and to optimize your channels.

Maybe you need to explain things differently on your website? Is your newsletter informative and valuable enough for your target customers? Or perhaps you notice that one channel is not working as well as you thought and want to test another. That's what this week is for. However, keep in mind that the channels have only been active for a short time, and some channels need a long lead time before they fulfill their purpose (e.g., a blog). So, don't give up too quickly, especially as some channels don't cost you any money or not much (see the table from day 61 to 65).

In the section "Further reading," I recommend in-depth sources that you can use according to your needs. If you use my email service, you'll receive an up-to-date list of further literature for each task.

Step 5:
Do only what you like and outsource the rest

Day 76 — Choose your company name

| 15 min. | 90-plus min. (on some days) | www.hes90.com/76 |

If your business idea is developing so well that you still believe in it, now is the time to take care of the infrastructure so that your business can grow and "mature."

Your business idea will determine what kind of infrastructure you need. In each of the following days, you'll deal with one foundational facet you'll need as an entrepreneur. I'll provide tips on how to secure it quickly and cheaply.

Here comes your task for today:

Your future company will typically need an official company name, and you'll certainly want to give your "baby" a striking name.

Maybe you already have an idea? If not, start thinking of a name today. Here are some general tips:

1. It should be clear how to pronounce the name when you read it or spell it when you hear it.

2. Choose a name that doesn't restrict you even as your business grows, for example, by being too specific.

3. Conduct thorough research on the Internet to discover what others call themselves and whether a competitor has already taken your idea.

4. Get the.org and/or.com domain for your name (or another domain that suits your target audience).

5. Conduct a trademark search for your name: https://www.uspto.gov. Think about whether the name is catchy.

6. Get feedback from at least ten different people.

7. Make sure that the name sounds great out loud.

8. Use tools for brainstorming names. Under the following link, you'll find ideas I've put together: www.how-employees-startup.com/find-a-name

Here you'll find terms related to English words in a visual form, or you can have name suggestions generated by specifying a term. So, "Yoga" becomes "NextDay Yoga," "Pioneer Yoga," "Yoga Central," "Live Yoga," etc.

9. Make sure that you are personally happy with the name. You'll have to live with the name for a long time, so take your time to get it right from the start.

Day 77 — Find the appropriate legal form

20 min.	60 min.	www.hes90.com/77	

After you started the process of finding a name yesterday, today you'll choose the appropriate corporate form for your business idea. I cannot give you any legal advice, so you'll have to consult a suitable lawyer. However, I would like to briefly introduce the most important forms in the US and their advantages and disadvantages.

Sole Proprietor

As its name implies, a sole proprietorship is a company owned and operated by a single person. If your business is not a corporation or limited company and you are the sole owner of your business, it is a sole proprietorship. As a sole proprietor, any business income you earn is considered personal income when you file your taxes. The downside of setting up your business this way is you are personally liable for any money your business owes and are personally vulnerable for any lawsuits filed against your business.

Limited Liability Company (LLC)

An LLC is a hybrid business that marries some of the features of a corporation with some of the features of a sole proprietorship. Unlike a sole proprietorship, if you are registered with the government as an LLC, your business assets and liabilities are legally separated from your personal assets and liabilities. Moreover, unlike a corporation, income you earn from your LLC is treated as personal income, just like it is if you are a sole proprietor.

General Partnership

A general partnership is a business arrangement by which two or more individuals agree to share in all assets, profits, and financial and legal liabilities of a jointly-owned business. In a general partnership, partners agree to unlimited liability, meaning liabilities are not capped and can be paid through the seizure of an owner's assets. Furthermore, any partner may be sued for the business's debts.

Each is responsible for their personal tax liabilities—including partnership earnings—on their income tax returns as taxes do not flow through the general partnership.

Limited Partnership

A limited partnership (LP)—not to be confused with a limited liability partnership (LLP)—is a partnership made up of two or more partners. The general partner oversees and runs the business while limited partners do not partake in managing the business. However, the general partner has unlimited liability for the debt, and any limited partners have limited liability up to the amount of their investment.

A limited partnership exists when two or more partners go into business together, but one or more of the partners are only liable up to the amount of their investment.

Cooperations

Incorporating means to create a corporation, which is the act of legally separating a business from yourself. It becomes a stand-alone entity that generates income and pays its shareholders and/or employees. There are a few varieties to choose from in the United States but since the chances are low that you want to start your business as a cooperation now I leave this to your advisors, that you then definitely need.

Effects of the choice of legal form

The legal form also impacts other factors, such as the **registration formalities** at the time of establishment, the necessary **initial capital**, etc. See the table below to choose the most appropriate legal form for you:

BUSINESS STRUCTURE ALTERNATIVES

Issues to consider	Sole proprietorship	C Corporation (Regular Corporation)	S Corporation (Sub-chapter S Corporation)	General Partnership	Limited partnership	Limited Liability Company (LLC)
Ownership Rules	One owner	Unlimited number of shareholders with no limit on the classes of stock	Up to 100 shareholders allowed One class of stock allowed	Unlimited number of general partners	Unlimited numbers of general and limited partners allowed	Unlimited number of "members" allowed
Liability of Owners	Unlimited liability for obligations of the business	Generally, no personal liability for obligations of the corporation	Generally, no personal liability for obligations of the corporation	All general partners fully liable for obligations of the business	Unlimited liability for the general partners and no personal liability for the limited partners	Generally, no personal liability for obligations of the entity
Federal Tax Treatment	Entity is not taxed, all income and losses passed through to owner	Corporation is taxed at the corporate level	Entity is not taxed; profits and losses are passed through to shareholders	Entity is not taxed, all income and losses passed through to partners	Entity is not taxed; profits and losses are passed through to general and limited partners	Entity is not taxed; profits and losses are passed through to members
Control and Management	Sole proprietor manages business	Board of Directors has overall management responsibility with officers having day-to-day responsibility	Board of Directors has overall management responsibility with officers having day-to-day responsibility	General partner(s) manages the business subject to the partnership agreement and officers may have day-to-day responsibility	General partner manages the business subject to the Limited Partnership Agreement	Board of Managers or members manage the business subject to the company operating agreement and officers have day-to-day responsibility
Capital Contributions	Sole proprietor makes any capital contributions as needed	Shareholders usually buy stock in the corporation. Corporation can issue common and preferred stock	Shareholders usually buy stock in the one class of stock issued by the corporation	General partners contribute money or services to business and receive interests in profits and losses	Both general and limited partners contribute money or services and receive interests in the profits and losses	The members typically contribute money or services to the LLC and receive an interest in the profits and losses
Ease of Establishing	Easiest	Must File Certificate of Formation with the Secretary of State	Must File Certificate of Formation with the Secretary of State	No filing. But a partnership agreement is needed	Must File Certificate of Formation with the Secretary of State	Must File Certificate of Formation with the Secretary of State

Figure 14: Business Structure Alternatives (Source: www.civil-law.com*)*

Day 78 — Design your company logo

20 min.	90 min.	www.hes90.com/78

Just as important as the name is a beautiful and catchy logo for your company. Logos can be created cheaply by artists on the Internet (from $5). You can find them here: www.how-employees-startup.com/logodesign.

Pay attention to the following aspects:

What makes a good logo?

A good logo is immediately recognizable, unmistakable, reflects your brand's message, and sets you apart from the competition. An effective logo looks timeless and professional and fits seamlessly into your brand identity. A good logo must also work in any size and wherever you want to use it.

But how do you get a nice and professional logo inexpensively if you're not a logo designer yourself or know one?

Here your task begins:

Find inspiration for your design by walking around your city or town with your eyes open, looking at websites, and — this probably helps best — by looking at the styles of logo designers on the logo design platforms at www.how-employees-startup.com/logodesign. That way, you might find the right designer for you.

Look at your competitors: How do others present themselves who offer the same or something similar?

Finally, decide on a **design style**.

Select the **color(s)** you want to use in your logo. Make sure that the colors match well and that the logo is easy to read, even from a distance.

Choose suitable **typography**, both for letters and words in your logo and for your company name. Your logo designer can also help you with this.

Find your **designer** on the web, for example, via www.how-employees-startup.com/logodesign and have several designs made in a competition and decide on your favorite.

Evaluate the logo designs and get a few people to provide multiple perspectives.

Here are some general questions you should ask yourself when creating and selecting logo options:

- Can people say what it is in two seconds? Will they immediately recognize from the logo what your company does?

- Is it simple and memorable?

- Is it versatile? Can it be applied to all your needs (e.g., in different media, color and black and white)?

- Is it timeless, or will it need a redesign in a few years because it so clearly reflects the current trend?

- Is it unique? Is it different from your competition?

- Does it appeal to your target audience?

Purpose of the logo

Think carefully about why and for what you need the logo. Your logo is your customers' first impression. Think of it as the image for a dating profile: it has to immediately resonate with the right people! It will be on your website, on your products, at your shop, on your flyers, etc. So, do it right!

Define your brand identity

The logo should communicate the personality of your company. What is it? What do you and your company stand for? Sustainability? Quality? Fun? Health? Authenticity? What makes you unique? Here you can access the results of Day 11 and Day 34, which is important to you.

Questions to further define your brand:

- Why do I want to set up this company?

- Which convictions and values are essential for my company and me?

- What do I do better than everyone else?

- What is my differentiator?

- If I had to describe my brand in just three words, what would they be?

- Which three words would I like to be described by my customers?

And now, have fun with this creative task! You are supposed to start the process today, but it'll probably take a few days before you complete it.

Printed matter and design

Despite the enormous importance of the Internet, printed matter is still an important medium for reaching, winning, and retaining customers. The costs for flyers, brochures, business cards, advertising banners, etc. are pleasantly low, so that you'll quickly have everything you need with little money. But again, make sure that you only print something when you are sure what, how much, and in what form you need. After all, there's a strong temptation to take care of something like business cards first, as they are a cheap and convincing expression of "I have a company."

The best way to have printed matter produced is to go to an online printing company. They offer you a website where you can choose from a variety of media. Next, upload your images and, if necessary, design the layout. You can also delegate this task to people who do it all the time. You just pay a few extra dollars for this.

Find suitable suppliers here: www.how-employees-startup.com/drucksachen They offer an unbelievable selection of printed materials that are also suitable as (later) advertising merchandise for your customers, such as mugs, bags, water bottles, and give you a professional appearance. Some service providers also offer overnight printing and free shipping. That is important if you want to test your business idea with a flyer, for example. Keep in mind that it's par for the course to modify your design based on your findings from previous experiments.

At www.how-employees-startup.com/logodesign, you'll find designers who can design the logo *and* marketing material, a book cover, etc. for as little as $50.

Day 79 — Open your (virtual) business space

🧍 25 min.	📋 90 min.	🌐 www.hes90.com/79	▪️ QR

Do you need your own shop (e.g., for a soup kitchen) or commercial space (e.g., for a copy shop) or a room (e.g., for a yoga studio) for your business idea?

Your task for today:

Look around for suitable premises to get a feel for the prices and put together the requirements you have for the property. In this way, you'll prepare what you need and what you'll have to pay for when your business is established later.

During this process, look for ways to realize your idea at a much lower cost. That will help minimize your costs, long-term obligations, and, thus, your risk for the time being. Here are a few suggestions:

- If you want to sell something in a shop, you can try renting a small corner **in an existing shop** first. For example, the same space can house a flower shop with a small CD shop and a vegan soup kitchen. Elsewhere, there is a comic book shop together with a tattoo studio and a clothing store. This way, you save money, have company, and benefit from existing customers. Of course, the customer segments must fit together well.

- If you need a professional kitchen to cook food for a delivery service, you can start by delivering only once a week and rent the kitchen from a **cooking school.**

- If you need an office, maybe only temporarily at the beginning, you can first work in a **co-working space.** Here there are so-called "hot desks," fixed workplaces (each per hour, day, week, or month), and separate offices (for weeks or months).

- If you would like to offer **courses** (e.g., yoga, sewing classes, lessons), you can often **rent a room** at a reasonable price from non-profit associations or at premises in the city. Here too, you can benefit from the existing clientele. For sports activities, parks are also suitable in summer, where yoga classes are often offered.

If you need an **address** for your business idea that appears to the outside world as your office, you should first use a virtual office and continue to work from home to save fixed costs in the initial period. At www.how-employees-startup.com/virtual-office, you'll find providers who offer you virtual office addresses in various large cities. You can use an office purely as a postal address, and you'll then receive the mail (from $99/month).

Or you can book the address as your official company headquarters and then, for example, add it to your website in the imprint (from $179/month).

Co-working Spaces

Co-working spaces are an ingenious invention of the 2010s. They can now be found in all medium-sized and large cities, often even a wide range of them. You can book a workplace in a co-working space by the hour, day, week, or month. There you'll find an inspiring environment with all the services you could wish for in an office (Internet, printer, fax, telephone service, drinks, relaxation areas, etc.) You'll also meet a lot of like-minded people, which not only motivates you and makes your work more enjoyable but often gives you a good network of potential partners, such as designers, programmers, marketing experts, etc. You can also rent meeting rooms or organize events where everything is taken care of. If you need an office for a longer period, you can also get your own room, which is already fully furnished. A significant advantage is that as you grow, you can often swap your office for a larger one without having to move address and phone number.

Here you can find an overview of the providers: www.how-employees-startup.com/coworking

Some small suppliers often operate only one single co-working space. These can be nice and intimate. Larger providers that operate worldwide offer their spaces in other cities or countries. That makes you feel at home anywhere in the world and is especially interesting if you travel a lot for your business idea. Just look up the providers in your area on the Internet and visit them one after the other. Allow each one to make you an offer right away so that you can compare and negotiate later.

In Hong Kong, I asked two employees to look at the top 10 that we'd selected together on the Internet. They then showed me their three favorites, and we visited them together. That way, I made sure that the rooms I chose also appealed to my staff.

Day 80 — Assign a (virtual) secretary

| | 20 min. | | 60 min. | | www.hes90.com/80 | |

For many business ideas, it's important to be easily accessible and to appear professional on the phone. Yet you are busy with all of your startup activities, and you might even be juggling working in your old profession. So, it can be beneficial if someone takes calls and handles correspondence for you, so that you don't have to be available continually and can concentrate on other tasks. There are secretarial services, virtual assistants, and call centers.

Your task today:

Have a look at the providers in the different categories and consider if and when you need them. Think about which services will help you concentrate on the tasks that are important to you. Be sure to test the service providers. Most of them offer a non-binding and free test phase. Feel free to test one, even if you don't (yet) need any services, just to get a feeling for what is possible today for little money and in high quality, to make your life easier and save a lot of time and money.

Virtual secretary

It's practical for many startups to **have** a **virtual secretary** who takes calls and passes on information when you're not available yourself.

You can also find suitable providers at www.how-employees-startup.com/virtual-office. There are different price scales, e.g., from $50/month or $.50 per minute.

Virtual secretaries is a fantastic invention because you can get started quickly for little money and still appear professional. They provide you with a telephone number and, if required, an address where you and "your office" can always be reached.

EXAMPLE: Let's assume you are Mike Brooks, and your company is called "Sun Consulting." If a customer calls "you," a member of the virtual office ("vOffice") answers in a professional and friendly voice:

vOffice: "Good afternoon, Sun Consulting, Patricia Miller speaking. What can I do for you?"

Caller: "Uh, hello, is Mr. Brooks available?"

vOffice: "Oh, I am sorry. Mr. Brooks is in a meeting right now. Can he call you back?"

Caller: "Yes, gladly. My name is Peter Smith, and my number is..."

vOffice: "Thank you very much, Mr. Smith. Could you tell me briefly what this is about? Then I'll let Mr. Brooks know."

Caller: "Yes, it's about a potential consulting assignment in the XXXX area, and we would like to receive an offer."

vOffice: "All right, Mr. Smith. I'll take care of it. Is there anything else I can do for you?"

Caller: "No, thanks, that's it. Goodbye. "

vOffice: "Goodbye, Mr. Smith, and have a nice day!

Mr. Smith hangs up and thinks: "Wow, I'd love to have a competent and friendly assistant like Mr. Brooks's. He must be busy and seems well organized. "

One minute later, you'll receive Mr. Smith's contact details and his request via the provider's app. You can then decide if and when you want to call him back yourself or if you want to delegate the call back to the virtual office, to your virtual assistant (see below), to your colleague, etc.

Some service providers also offer you official postal addresses, if required, in well-known locations that stand for exclusivity (e.g., Silicon Valley or New York's financial district). In addition, you can rent offices and meeting rooms of various sizes by the hour if required.

Virtual assistants

If virtual secretarial services and offices are new to you, the next one may leave you speechless. For little money, you can hire a personal assistant who can organize and take care of all sorts of things for you via phone, mail, and the Internet. These so-called "virtual assistants" live and work in countries where wages are significantly lower than in Europe or North America, such as India, China, Bangladesh, the Philippines, etc. Here you can get well-qualified people for $5 to $10/hour for tasks that you do not want to or cannot do yourself. However, the most important thing is that you explain the job well and do a few test-runs with your potential assistant before engaging them for a more extended period and giving them more responsibility.

A list of virtual assistant providers can also be found at: www.how-employees-startup.com/virtual-office.

You can hire a particular person, with the advantage that you get to know each other better, who will be familiar with your requirements. You can also hire a team, with one person as your contact, who will delegate the task to different people on their team. The disadvantage is that it may be a little more expensive, and the quality of the results may vary depending on the person. The advantage, however, is that you don't suddenly have to look for a new assistant if yours is unable to work or changes jobs, which can happen quickly.

You don't have to worry about being morally reprehensible with the relatively low hourly wage. These jobs are much more attractive by local standards than other jobs. As a result, labor costs increase over time, so you are actually helping rather than harming the positive income development in these countries.

Call center

For some business models, it's essential that customers can reach you at any time. You'll hardly want to set up and operate your own call center for this purpose, so here too, you'll fall back on a service provider who offers you everything from a single source. There's a distinction between active (outbound: the call center initiates the call) and passive (inbound: the call center answers the call).

Call centers are particularly useful for the following tasks:

- Information purposes — as a hotline for product information
- Customer service and complaint management
- Market research
- Sale with conclusion of contract
- Order and order acceptance
- Emergency services

You can also find providers for call center services at: www.how-employees-startup.com/virtual-office.

Days 81 and 82 — Incorporate your company

15 min.	90 min.	www.hes90.com/81	

During this week, you'll set up your company according to the requirements resulting from the legal form you have chosen.

Your task today and tomorrow:

Compile the necessary documents and, if necessary, seek further advice from an expert. Perhaps there's someone in your circle of acquaintances? Maybe your tax consultant can help you.

Otherwise, contact the Chamber of Commerce responsible for your city (https://www.uschamber.com/co/chambers) and arrange a consultation appointment.

Then submit the documents, i.e., register your business in the desired legal form.

Day 83 — Choose you accounting solution

15 min.   90 min.   www.hes90.com/83

Even if it's rather annoying and uncomfortable for most entrepreneurs: You must take care of necessary administrative details from the very beginning: bookkeeping, invoicing, business account, tax consultant, etc. Today, we start with the core of the business: accounting. If you are not a trained accountant, leave it to the professionals.

Here is your task for today:

Find either a tax office that does the accounting or an online solution. These are now well-established and offer a low-cost start from $7.00 per month.

You can find an overview of providers here: www.how-employees-startup.com/bookkeeping.

You can also combine both, i.e., doing your own accounting with an online solution, but use a tax advisor who takes care of the taxes and advises you. In this way, you save costs on bookkeeping but have someone at your side who can point out mistakes or options that can help you save a lot of money and trouble.

Day 84 — Open your business account

	15 min.		60 min.		www.hes90.com/84

At some point, you'll need a business account for your independence. If you don't make many and/or expensive purchases for your business idea and don't have any revenue yet, you can still use your private account. However, if you are already confident that you'll continue on the path to self-employment, you can open a business account now.

Your task today:

Find a bank you trust and apply today to open your business account. But don't be surprised: if you've only had a private account in the past, you'll be surprised at all the fees you have to pay with a business account, for example, for every transfer. Not all providers offer a business account for all legal forms. Think about whether you need to have a local contact person (e.g., Wells Fargo, Chase Bank, U.S. Bank, and other branch banks) or whether you prefer a direct bank without branches like Ally Bank or even one of the modern fintechs (combine technology or financial services) such as PayPal or Venmo.

You can find a current overview of providers here: www.how-employees-startup.com/bank.

It also depends a bit on your business idea: If you offer something locally, the local banks have the advantage because they can help you with their network if necessary. If your business idea is an online business, the direct banks or fintechs may be more suitable.

By the way, the price should not be your main criterion for choosing a business account. Other critical knock-out factors when selecting a bank include: Is your legal form supported? How do you get cash when you need it? Does the bank also offer financing for future growth or just payment transactions? Other factors include the trust the bank enjoys with you, how quickly and easily you can open the business account and whether you need additional features that some banks offer, such as financial planners, billing software, or accounting.

Day 85 — Launch your website

5 min.	90 min. + more over next weeks/months	www.hes90.com/85	

Almost every business has a website these days, and chances are that one will be worth your while. Why? Because nowadays almost everyone is looking for providers on the Internet. Also, the Internet is the perfect channel to attract customers who are *not* looking for you because they don't know they need your offer. Online marketing (e.g., Google Ads or Facebook Ads) can help you reach your customer group quickly and accurately — but it also costs a lot, as explained below.

Apps are also becoming increasingly popular and are now relatively easy to create. However, you should already have a good reason to offer an app and what your customers should do with it.

The methods to own an app or website are diverse and offer distinct advantages and disadvantages.

Here is your task for today:

Here I present three options, depending on your needs and budget. Think about whether and when you want to invest in a website and decide on a suitable provider.

Web domain and web hosting

Most of the companies that design a website for you are also happy to take care of domain registration and web hosting. Of course, you have to pay for it yourself because the hosting with the domain usually costs a monthly fee. The registration of the domain often causes one-time costs, but these are not very high.

A simple website for little money or even free

If your business idea does not refer to the Internet itself, but you want to use the Internet as a digital business card on which your (potential) customers can inform themselves, you need a classic website. These are already available today for very little money or even for free.

If you want to do things yourself to save money and get the first result quickly, there are simple solutions I have put together for you here: www.how-employees-startup.com/website.

Regardless of whether it's a website with information, a blog, or an online shop, you'll find proven providers for all areas.

A simple app for little money

Meanwhile, several online tools allow you to build your own app based on a "template" without any programming knowledge. You can use this as a great jumping-off point when discussing your ideas with a professional developer.

You should be aware of the two basic forms of apps:

- **Progressive Web Apps** (PWA) are a mobile phone-friendly website opened on a smartphone, as well as a tablet and PC/laptop via a browser.

- **Native Apps** are the small applications that you download from an App Store and install as icons on your iPhone or Android phone. These are a bit more sophisticated and usually more expensive to develop than PWAs. Most users want Native Apps.

You can find an overview of providers of apps at: www.how-employees-startup.com/apps.

A progressive web app costs about $25 per month, native Android apps cost $48 per month, and iOS apps for Apple iPad and iPhone cost almost $100 per month. But some providers are completely free, who earn their money by advertising in your app.

A somewhat more sophisticated app or website that is to be maintained and developed in the future

If your website is an integral part of your business idea or you even want to sell over the Internet, the requirements are usually a bit higher. In this case, it makes sense to look for a competent partner to build up your website and maintain it for you.

If you think you can do it, it makes sense to first create a simple app or website yourself with the above-mentioned providers. This costs very little money, and, over time, you'll learn what you actually need. Should you include a blog? Do you want customers to be able to register for a newsletter? Would a chat be useful? When you're finished with the structure of your app or website, find an expert who will develop it more professionally according to your wishes to make the design more striking and add functions not available in the cheap "construction kits."

Here you'll find an overview of providers who develop and maintain a professional website for you: www.how-employees-startup.com/website.

If you would like to use a partner, find one who makes a good impression on you and get an offer without stating a price limit. In return, you'll explain to him what you have in mind, and he'll ask you questions about points you have not thought of. Step-by-step, this will give you a clearer picture of your app or website, and you'll receive an offer. Anticipate an expensive offer because we haven't set a limit (deliberately).

However, do not accept this offer under any circumstances yet, but get at least two comparison offers, this time setting a limit which is significantly lower than the first offer (e.g., $500 instead of the $1,500 demanded by the first offer). The preparation of the offers will now be much faster, as the most important requirements have already been clarified. In the conversations with the other providers, you'll now determine whether they're more competent (e.g., by asking you important questions that the other one didn't even have) or whether your first choice was perhaps the right one. If the first provider still appeals to you the most, talk to them about the comparison offers and tell them that you would like to work with them but that you have significantly cheaper offers. As a rule, they will offer you the competitor's price. If not, it's up to you whether you hire him after all and invest more money. If they don't give in too quickly and not too much, this can be a good sign. It could well be that they are worth more money.

In any case, be guided by how much you trust the individual. If you have a bad feeling, by all means, leave it and keep looking. There are an incredible number of suppliers out there who would love to have your business.

At the providers under www.how-employees-startup.com/website, you'll find a wide variety of service providers, including many web and app developers. The costs range from $100 for a very simple website or app to several thousand or tens of thousands of dollars for something more sophisticated.

A very sophisticated app or website that is the heart of your business

If the website or app is the core of your business, it might be worth looking for a partner near you. This has the great advantage that you can get together to discuss your requirements, eliminating potential miscommunications that can arise from virtual interactions. Your partner will present interim results and clarify any newly emerging questions with you. Such a partner is easily five to ten times more expensive than one on the other side of the world. But communication can be so crucial to success or failure that it pays off.

You can find professional providers in your area via the portals mentioned above by entering your region in the search or via Google search. Consider whether you have an IT-savvy friend or acquaintance who can support you at the beginning and accompany you during the initial discussions and meetings. This person could save you a lot of time and money by acting as a "bridge" between you and your business idea and the IT world at the beginning.

Online Marketing

Online marketing includes all advertising activities carried out online, i.e., advertising on websites, apps, newsletters, advertising e-mails, and advertising on social networks. This is a separate and very complex area where you either already know your way around (in which case I don't need to explain much) or don't. In the latter case, you don't want to learn this to build your business because this is a science in itself. The good news is that many freelancers around the world are happy to do this job for you.

As described above, you can also find them on one of the platforms: www.how-employees-startup.com/website.

Step 6:
Scale your business to the right size for you

Days 86 to 88 — Take your new life into your own hands!

5 min.	30 min.	www.hes90.com/86	

Isn't it incredible!? Today, the last working week of the 90-Day Program begins! You've actually made it this far! Maybe you're so "in" by now that you don't even need the help of my program anymore? If so, then I'm all the more pleased because that is and was my goal: that you can tank up so much self-confidence, gain so much experience and confidence during the program that you can manage on your own. You are never really alone; you have your friends, family, acquaintances, and your network. This will also help you in the future, especially if you continue to consciously pay attention to getting together with people who are good for you, do not rob you of energy, and like you just the way you're.

This week is all about preparing for the big step of leaving your old job — if you want to — and getting fully involved in your new future. There are a few things to consider before saying "goodbye" to your old job and making a good transition to your new "job." You'll be responsible for organizing the tasks yourself this week because you know best when what fits best. Here are a few suggestions as to what might be useful this week:

First task for this week:

Your aim should be to part with your old employer, boss, and colleagues in the most positive way possible. Now is not the time to settle scores, right the wrongs, or burn bridges. Remember: You are not responsible for changing others. Be happy that you're leaving soon and allow the people who stay behind to live their lives. Remember, you never know what role your colleagues may play in the future. Make your departure optimistic; it's their last impression of you. And who knows — maybe this impression will be meaningful for you in the future after all.

Second task for this week:

Recheck your company's resignation policy and prepare your notice of termination in compliance with those guidelines to avoid misunderstandings and leave an overall positive impression.

Submit your notice of resignation in due time to be free on your desired date. Some companies release employees immediately upon notice of resignation with pay. This would be ideal, of course, because you'd have a salary for the remaining time, while fully focusing on developing your business idea.

In any case, discuss your resignation with your boss first, even if the relationship is not good. This way, you've conducted yourself professionally and fairly. Wait for a good time and give them an indirect warning: "Boss, I'd like to discuss something important and personal with you. When's a good time for you?" That way, he can already smell the roast, so he won't be caught off-guard. Then explain to him in clear, simple, and neutral terms that you're going to resign to take on a new job and would like to inform him first and in advance before you submit your written notice.

Complete your job responsibilities to the best of your ability to ensure a smooth transition for your colleagues or clients. Again, a professional and responsible attitude is better for you in the long run.

I strongly encourage avoiding discussion of your job/company's negative aspects when asked about why you're resigning. Leave all of that behind you. Instead, talk about the positive things that lie ahead, for example: "I've felt more and more strongly lately that I want to do something different, and I've finally found the courage to take the step." If you like, you can explain briefly what you're planning to do. Who knows? Maybe you'll find a new customer or someone who'll consider you a role model and also want to build something of their own.

Here's a possible formulation: If your relationship with your supervisor was acceptable:

"In the years here at (company name), I felt very comfortable. I had the opportunity to acquire new knowledge and develop skills, and I'm very grateful for that. I now have the opportunity to work in another position that is very close to my interests and where I can still grow. After careful consideration, I've decided to take this opportunity. Therefore, I'd like to discuss how best utilize the rest of my time here for a smooth transition."

If your relationship wasn't so good and your boss asks why you're leaving, answer evasively:

"The current work environment had no bearing on my decision to leave. The new job is a better fit for my current interests and skills."

Third task for this week:

If it suits you, thank your colleagues and superiors with a small going-away party.

Additional helpful questions to ensure you've covered all bases:

- ✔ Who do you've to give your notice to?
- ✔ How can you make the transition smooth for both sides?
- ✔ Who do you've to talk to about your job reference, and should you pre-formulate it if necessary?
- ✔ Which tasks and projects do you still want to complete?
- ✔ Which colleagues, customers, and partners should you inform? How are they informed, and by whom?
- ✔ Do you've backup copies of important data?
- ✔ Are all open questions answered and responsibilities clarified?
- ✔ Are there any agreements directly related to your high-level access to company/ client data?
- ✔ In which tasks do you want to personally train your successor(s)?

Use the week to clarify these issues and the next weeks to plan the handovers.

Day 89 — Professionalize your Company

👤 15 min.   📋 90 min.   🌐 www.hes90.com/89

You have now almost completed the 90-Day Program. Today is the penultimate day! In the meantime, you've already developed yourself and your idea to such an extent that it's no longer possible to give you concrete tips on what to do on a daily basis. Therefore, I would like to offer my top 18 tips today, which will save you a lot of trouble and money as you progress:

1. Take out private **pension insurance** and make sure it is protected in the event of insolvency.

2. Always make written **contracts**, even if you loan your company funds from your private assets. Remember: contracts are there *now* so that you don't need them later.

3. Try to remain a **sole proprietorship** if possible, i.e., do not set up a partnership, as the requirements are often lower and the regulations easier to understand.

4. Ensure that you adhere to the **formal requirements** according to your chosen legal form, for example, complete invoice numbers, produce your own receipts for issues without receipts, data protection requirements, customs clearance, etc. Not doing this will be expensive, frustrating, and will cause sleepless nights.

5. Get a **tax adviser** early on, with whom you'll get on well personally. There are so many administrative pitfalls — you cannot and do not want to know all of them. Again, concentrate on what you *want* to do and absolutely *have* to do yourself and look for suitable partners for everything else.

6. You need **clean bookkeeping, account management, cash management, and cost accounting** from the very beginning. Discuss this with your tax consultant and find a service provider for this. Any carelessness here will be expensive and very painful later on.

7. **Avoid hiring employees** for as long as possible, as this can lead to a whole host of liability and tax problems that make your life as a business owner more difficult. It's great to create jobs, and it's nice when you can do that, but avoid it until you've reached a critical size and gained adequate experience. It's no help to anyone if you get sick from worrying about how to pay your monthly salaries and put a strain on yourself and your family. Instead, use self-employed

people like yourself, service providers, temporary employment agencies, fixed-term contracts, etc.

8. Beware of **cheats**. If you register your new business (e.g., in the commercial register) or apply for a trademark, you're 100% certain to receive unsolicited letters from companies that charge fees for services you've never ordered and do not need. The letters look like they came from a public authority. They have received your details because a new entry has been made in an official database. Read such letters carefully and search for the slightest doubt about which "provider" is behind them.

9. Make sure that you — or your partners who create something for you — observe the law on the small **formalities** so that you do not involuntarily become the victim of a warning issued by professional warning companies. Examples are an incomplete legal notice on your website, incorrect use of copyrighted sources (e.g., photos and images), missing mandatory information in commercial emails, newsletters, spam, advertising law, competition law, etc.

10. Collect payment upfront, if possible, to avoid multiple annoyances and costs from reminders and the like.

11. Take advantage of resources provided by local and national **chambers of commerce,** BNI (Business Network International, SBC (Small Business Development Center), your local Economic Development office, etc. if you have them, and even more so if you're a compulsory member of them. Make an appointment to get to know them, explain what you do, and ask how they can support you. If you have a question, go to them first before you pay someone to answer it. They are there for you! There are many different and potentially valuable and useful resources not used by many because of ignorance.

12. **Start your business by yourself** and avoid partners, if possible. It may be reassuring and be more fun to share joys and sorrows with someone. However, in practice, it turns out that sole proprietorships are easier to do while avoiding challenges with relationships and emotions. What may be an advantage in the startup phase can quickly become a disadvantage when it comes to day-to-day operations.

13. As a self-employed person, take care of **health insurance, retirement, nursing care, and social security in** good time. The minimum contribution to private health insurance is high, even more so when you're older or have a family. In addition, you often have to prepay for medical costs, which puts a strain on your cashflow.

14. One of the most common stumbling blocks for the self-employed is a **tax payment** that often comes years later and is much higher than expected. A

critical tip: set up your own bank account for tax payments, into which you always pay 30% of your estimated profit. You should also report any drop in profits directly to the tax office, as they will estimate your tax burden based on your profits in recent years.

15. Save yourself the trouble of **filing a patent**. This is expensive because you absolutely need a patent attorney as it's far too complicated to do it yourself. Also, it's very unlikely patents will legally protect you since there are many ways to avoid a patent, the other side might have the better lawyers etc. Patents can be useful for advertising or as a deterrent to imitators. But there might be even easier, faster, and cheaper ways to achieve this.

16. Regularly **backup your data**. It rarely happens, but once all the data is gone, the stress is great, and the work enormous. Buy an external hard drive and make a backup at least once a month using your operating system's standard backup function.

17. Define an **abort criterion for your independence**. Challenges are inherent in any startup, and you shouldn't give up immediately when things get difficult and remember: a successful startup also takes time. That said, set a realistic timeframe and target criterion at which you'll stop trying to set up your own business. Tell people you trust about this and ask them to question you at the appropriate time. For example: "If I don't earn the running costs at the very minimum in a year, i.e., on 9/30/21, I will give up. And, if after two years, i.e., on 9/30/22, I don't make at least $1,000 a month in profits, I'll discontinue the business." Avoid turning an end with horror into a horror without end.

Day 90 — Today is the first day of the rest of your life

5 min.	lifetime	www.hes90.com/90

Today is the last day of your 90-Day Program and the first day of the rest of your life! There is nothing to do today except to acknowledge what you've accomplished over the past weeks and months! And I would like to thank you for your trust, commitment, and loyalty.

Here is your task for today:

Look back again at what you've done and accomplished — honor that. Celebrate yourself! And please write me a short email about how you've been doing. I will definitely read it and answer you. I will use your feedback to constantly improve this programm so that future self-employed people will find it even easier. You can reach me at: moritz@ how-employees-startup.com.

I wish you all the best on your journey, success with your business idea, and the right priorities for your life. Always remember that it is the little things that make life beautiful, that time is much more valuable than (more) money, and that it is the experiences with ourselves and the people we love that make for happiness, joy, and truly living life.

Best wishes and all the best!

Yours sincerly,
Moritz

Acknowledgements

This book was written after a time in which I needed and received a lot of support. I would like to thank all those who have contributed to the success of this book.

First of all, there is my wife Zsuzsanna, the love of my life, and my sons Theo and Felix. Thank you for being there for me, no matter how good or bad I feel.

I thank all the "guinea pigs" who tested the 90-Day Program, the friends and relatives who gave me feedback on the manuscript and the 220 supporters of my Kickstarter campaign who helped me in the creation of this book. You know who you are and can hardly imagine how motivating your contributions were for me and what a significant part each of you played in making this book a success!

The book became only so beautiful thanks to the active support of Melanie Krieger and Oliver Hums from Metropolitan Verlag, the beautiful illustrations by Michael Schrenk, the editing by Julie Sykora, and the layout by Alexey Zgola.

Everything I know I have learned from others. For this I would like to thank the founders, co-founders and start-ups with whom I have been able to work over the last 15 years. As representatives, I would like to mention Maximilian Suermann from Großstadtzwerge Berlin, Stefan Schmidt from Unibright.io and Dimitri Gärtner from Framen.io.

I owe the fact that I was able to write this book without quitting my job to my dear colleagues at Zühlke Engineering, the best employer in the world. Thank you very much for your support over the last 10 years!

And finally, I would like to thank you, dear reader, for buying and reading this book and — I hope — working through the 90-day program. I would be so happy to hear from you and your experiences with it.

Thank you very much!

About the Author

Dr. Moritz Gomm is a serial entrepreneur, startup coach, and innovation consultant. As a graduate in business IT, he taught and received his doctorate from the chair of business management at the Technical University of Darmstadt.

Moritz has been coaching startups and sole proprietors for more than 15 years and is on the advisory board of various tech startups. He has been working as an innovation consultant for companies for more than a decade and has, among other things, developed Rent-a-Startup®, a method by which established companies implement radically new business ideas.

In 2018, he established Zühlke Engineering HK Ltd, an innovation service provider in Hong Kong. He has also lived in Thailand, Malaysia, and China. Today he lives in Darmstadt (Germany) with his wife and two sons.

For more support on how to successfully start your own business go to:

www.how-employees-startup.com

Further Reading

Ware, Bronnie (2019): Top Five Regrets of the Dying: A Life Transformed by the Dearly Departing. Hay House.

Deci, E. R./Ryan, R. M. (2008): Self-Determination Theory: A Macrotheory of Human Motivation, Development and Health, S. 183. In: Canadian Psychology 49, 182–185.

Guillebeau, Chris (2016): The $100 Startup: Reinvent the Way You Make a Living, Do What You Love, and Create a New Future

Ferriss, Timothy (2007): The 4-Hour Work Week.

Gassmann, Oliver (2017): Developing Business Models: 55 Innovative Concepts with the St. Gallen Business Model Navigator. 2nd ed. Carl Hanser Publishing House.

Gulder, Angelika (2013): Finde den Job, der dich glücklich macht. Von der Berufung zum Beruf. Campus. (German book)

Kasser, T./Ryan, R. M. (1993): A Dark Side of the American Dream: Correlates of Financial Success as a Central Life Aspiration. Journal of Personality and Social Psychology, 65(2), 410–422. — https://doi.org/10.1037/0022-3514.65.2.410

Krznaric, Roman (2012): How to Find Fulfilling Work. The School of Life. Pan Macmillan, Hamshire

Maurya, A. (2012): Running Lean. Iterating from Plan A to Plan That Works. 2nd Edition, O'Reilly, Cambridge.

Osterwalder, Alexander/Pigneur, Yves/Clark, Tim: (2010): Business Model Generation: A Handbook for Visionaries, Game Changers, and Challengers. Strategyzer series Wiley, Hoboken.

Reiss, Steven (2009): The Reiss Profile: The 16 Motives of Life. Which values and needs underly our behavior. Gabal publishing house.

Ries, Eric (2017): The Lean Startup: How Today's Entrepreneurs Use Continuous Innovation to Create Radically Successful Businesses. Currency Publishing.

End Notes

1   Brené Brown in the TED Talk "Listening to Shame" www.youtube.com/watch?v=psN1DORYYV0

2   Zukunftsinstitut in its white paper Die Zukunft nach Corona (2020), p. 8. ("The future after Corona").

3   Steve Jobs in his speech for graduates of Stanford University. — www.youtube.com/watch?v=D1R-jKKp3NA

4   Krznaric (2012).

5   Ferriss (2007).

6   https://tim.blog/2020/02/06/brene-brown-striving-self-acceptance-saving-marriages/

7   www.nature.com/articles/s41562-017-0277-0.epdf

8   This story is told over and over again and the original author is unknown to me. I have this story from Ferriss, T. (2007).

9   Ware (2019)

10   According to the self-determination theory (SDT) by Deci/Ryan (2008).

11   Eckstein (2015) has adopted this metaphor.

12   https://de.statista.com/themen/101/medien/ and http://web.ard.de/ard-chronik/index/12220?year=2019&month=10 (in German).

13   https://www.shopify.com/blog/what-is-dropshipping.

14   Interview with Jochen Mai — www.zeit.de/karriere/beruf/2014-02/interview-vom-bloggen-leben (in German).

15   https://www.zeit.de/karriere/beruf/2014-02/interview-vom-bloggen-leben (in German).

16   www.franchise.org (homepage of the International Franchise Association (IFA).

17   The example is taken from the highly recommended www.franchise.org book by Guilder, A. (2013). (German book)

18   Ries (2014).

19   Maurya (2012).

20   Osterwalder/Pigneur/Clark *(2010)*.

21   Ries (2014).

22   Book Icon made by www.flaticon.com/authors/freepik; To-Do Icon made by www.flaticon.com/authors/smashicons; Web Icon made www.flaticon.com/authors/kiranshastry.

23   This task is inspired by Gulder (2013).

24   www.youtube.com/watch?v=D1R-jKKp3NA.

25   www.niu.edu/facdev/_pdf/guide/learning/howard_gardner_theory_multiple_intelligences.pdf.

26   e.g., https://link.springer.com/article/10.1023/A:1014411319119 or Kasser/Ryan (1993). — https://doi.org/10.1037/0022-3514.65.2.410.

Printed in Great Britain
by Amazon

29866385R00132